D0551484

FOSTER'S
SCOTTISH
ODDITIES

FOSTER'S SCOTTISH ODDITIES

Allen Foster

BLACK & WHITE PUBLISHING

First published 2010
by Black & White Publishing Ltd
29 Ocean Drive, Edinburgh EH6 6JL

1 3 5 7 9 10 8 6 4 2   10 11 12 13

ISBN: 978 1 84502 288 4

Typeset by Ellipsis Books Limited, Glasgow
Printed and bound by MPG Books Ltd, Bodmin, Cornwall

Contents

Introduction

Foster's Scottish Oddities is a collection of strange Scottish trivia. It's a bit like a Scottish version of the wonderful *Ripley's Believe It or Not!* books that were once extremely popular. Robert Ripley travelled the world looking for strange facts. I made do looking through old books, newspapers and archives in various libraries and online. If you like this book, you will love the *Fortean Times* (www.forteantimes.com), a monthly magazine dedicated to the weird and unusual.

Painstaking efforts have been made to ensure that all the bizarre trivia within *Foster's Scottish Oddities* are correct. In a book with so many facts, it would be hard to believe that some errors have not been made. If you spot any mistakes or would like to contribute any strange facts, please send them to the author c/o Black & White Publishing.

Jonathan Williams, Doug Ferris, everyone at Black & White Publishing and many other unsung heroes deserve credit for their part in this book's creation.

To my Mother and Father

Amazing Feats

FOR a small wager, on 9 October 1792, a painter in Kelso called McGregor bet that he could fell a bullock with his fist in three punches. He did it at the second blow. What makes his feat more remarkable is that McGregor was of slight build and only five feet, seven inches tall.

• • •

THE Dundee steamer *William Hope* was driven on to the rocky shores of Aberdour Bay in Fife and wrecked on the night of 27 October 1884 when its engines failed during a storm. John and Jane Whyte and their nine children lived only a short distance from the shore of the bay in Waukmill, a small woollen mill and croft. After her husband had left for work the following morning, Jane went down to the shore for a walk with her collie. A short distance from the shore she spotted the half-sunken wreck of the *William Hope* in the raging sea. Men stranded on the wreck were clinging to the masts. They cried out to Jane Whyte for help.

One of the survivors threw her a rope and she braved the bitterly cold and dangerous seas to reach the rope. Somehow she managed to tie it around her waist and get back to shore.

There was nothing on shore on which to tie the rope in order to anchor it, so Jane held the line tight as all fifteen of the surviving crew men escaped the wreck and made it ashore through the heavy seas, aided by the rope. She took the cold and weary sailors home, dried their clothes and fed them. The next day they made their way back to Dundee, grateful to be alive. For her heroic actions, Jane Whyte was presented with the silver medal of the Royal Navy Lifeguard Institute and awarded £10.

• • •

TREVOR Robinson drank 100 cups of tea in nine hours fifty-six minutes on 4 May 1974, to claim a new world record for tea-drinking. While Robinson was delighted with the record, he said, 'I feel terrible.' The thirty-seven-year-old was a chief petty officer at the Faslane Royal Navy submarine base on Gare Loch, Dunbartonshire. His record attempt was made in an effort to raise money for charity. Each cup held one-third of a pint of hot, milky tea.

• • •

JOHN Henderson (1686–1758), a shipmaster from Borrowstounness, Lothian, and later its harbourmaster, was exceptionally devout. Every Sunday he fasted from morning until night and attended four public prayer meetings, then worshipped privately at least seven times throughout the day.

• • •

AT the age of sixty-two, Seamus McSporran retired from all fourteen of his jobs on the Isle of Gigha in the Inner Hebrides in April 2000. Since 1965 he had worked as a postmaster, shopkeeper, rent collector, police officer, fire chief, insurance agent, undertaker, pier master and registrar of births, marriages and deaths. McSporran also was the island's ambulance, bus and taxi driver – using the same vehicle – and ran a bed and breakfast. The island has a population of about 150 people.

• • •

HECTOR Lindsay (1859–1940) from Granton, Edinburgh, ran away from home at an early age and lived an adventurous life in many parts of the world for the rest of his days. We are fortunate that Lindsay wrote an autobiography, *Jungle Lindsay*, in 1936. While on an expedition in West Africa, Lindsay and thirty other men were captured by a tribe of cannibals. One by one they killed and ate his companions, but the tribe spared Lindsay's life when they saw the many tattoos all over his body. The tribe was in awe of Lindsay. They adopted him into their tribe and he lived several years with them before he managed to escape.

• • •

MARJORY Fleming (1803–11) from Kirkcaldy, Fife, was an extraordinary child prodigy who left poems, letters and a diary which are now one of the treasures of the National Library of Scotland. She died of meningitis at the age of eight.

• • •

IN the 1950s, Rev. D.T. Lauderdale of Lexington, Virginia, won the first prize of $5,000 in a *Ripley's Believe It or Not!*

competition to suggest the strangest oddity. He sent in the tale of a blind and armless Scottish man who was able to read with the tip of his tongue. William McPherson was born in Inverness in 1866 and immigrated to America with his wife in 1883. He was working in a Colorado stone quarry when a charge of dynamite exploded prematurely, leaving McPherson blind and armless. In time, in order to overcome his terrible disability, he learned to read with his tongue. While he pressed his tongue to raised dots representing letters, his teacher traced the letters on the bare skin of his back at a point between his shoulder-blades. In time he could read a book and turn its pages as fast as anyone and often remarked on how happy he was, despite his injuries. Thanks to the Reverend Lauderdale, McPherson was delighted to win the considerable prize money.

• • •

THE Reverend Hugh Smith (b.1812) from Irvine, Strathclyde, was from a poor background, but that did not stop him from getting on in life. Smith financed his entire education at

Glasgow University with the earnings from the sale of a single book of poetry, *Poetical Miscellany of Morals and Religion* (1832).

• • •

LIKE the Dutch boy of legend who used his hand as a water plug, a Scottish youth saved seven fishermen's lives by using his hand to plug a hole in a boat while the others rowed it to safety in the midst of a storm. Captain Archibald Ritchie of the vessel *Rose Hearty* gave the order to abandon ship on the night of 12 February 1931 after the engine had caught fire. The ship was off the west coast of Scotland at the time and all the crew's effort to extinguish the fire had failed.

The crew, consisting of Captain Ritchie, his five sons, his brother and a sixteen-year-old boy, were forced to take to a small boat. The plug in the bottom of the boat was missing, so Captain Ritchie's son John jammed his hand in the hole and kept it there for more than two hours while the others rowed and bailed the storm-tossed craft through the darkness. A nearby boat eventually spotted the flames from the fiery wreck of the *Rose Hearty* and came to the men's rescue.

• • •

JAMES Bruce from Kinnaird House, Larbert, Stirlingshire, was a famous explorer who spent several years travelling across uncharted parts of Africa, searching for the source of the Nile. On his return to London, Bruce and the stories he told were deemed to be so outlandish that he was widely regarded as a fraud. When he published an account of his travels in Africa in 1790, it was ridiculed as nonsense by scholars and other travellers. Over time the accuracy of Bruce's account was verified and his critics silenced. Ironically, after surviving many perils on his explorations, Bruce died at the age of sixty-four, after falling down the steps of his home on 27 April 1794.

• • •

COLIN Maclaurin (1698–1746) was a child prodigy from Kilmodan, Argyllshire.

He entered the University of Glasgow at age eleven and graduated three years later. He remained in the university to study divinity until 1717. Then he was elected Professor of Mathematics at the Marischal College in the University of Aberdeen at the age of nineteen years and eleven months, becoming the youngest person up till that time to hold a professorship. Maclaurin held this record as the world's youngest professor until March 2008 when New Yorker Alia Sabur was appointed a mathematics professor at Kankurk University in Seoul, South Korea, just a few days before she turned nineteen.

• • •

THE longest recorded ride in armour is one of 208 miles by fifty-eight-year-old Dick Brown, who rode from Edinburgh to his hometown of Dumfries. Brown set out on 10 June 1989 and arrived in Dumfries three days and six hours later. His total riding time was thirty-five hours and twenty-five minutes. The armour weighed fifty-eight pounds and Brown had to be lifted on to his horse with a winch, because he was so heavy.

• • •

ALEXANDER Selkirk (1676–1721) from Largo in Fife was the real Robinson Crusoe. In October 1704, afraid the ship he was sailing on was not seaworthy, Selkirk asked to be put ashore on the uninhabited island of Más a Tierra, 600 miles off South America. At the last moment, Selkirk changed his mind and begged to be taken back on board, but the cruel captain refused and sailed away. Selkirk spent the next four years and four months alone on the island, until he was rescued in February 1709. All he had to aid his survival was a musket, gunpowder, carpenter's tools, a knife, a Bible and some clothing. When the ship returned to Britain, Selkirk was interviewed by journalist Richard Steele, who published an article in *The Englishman* on 1 December 1713. Inspired by Selkirk's story – he may even have met him – Daniel Defoe published *Robinson Crusoe* in 1719.

• • •

AFTER flying solo across the Atlantic in a single-engine plane, American pilot Everett Hughes landed in a field 50 miles away from Glasgow on 30 July 1967. His tank was near empty. Hughes hitch-hiked to the nearest service station, purchased fuel, then flew on to Glasgow to continue his flight to Bitburg, West Germany, where he was an instructor at a military flying club. His route had taken him from the United States, via Canada, Greenland and Iceland, to Scotland.

• • •

IN 1735, Count de Buckeburg, a German visitor to Britain, wagered that he could ride a horse backwards from London to Edinburgh in four days. The horse's head was turned to Edinburgh, and the count sat backwards facing London. He completed the journey in 3 days and 20 hours and arrived in Edinburgh to a warm welcome from curious onlookers.

• • •

ACCORDING to James Russell, in his book *Reminiscences of Yarrow* (1894), the Reverend Alexander Johnston (1686–1788) of Lyne and Megget, Peeblesshire, preached a three-hour sermon every week for sixty years until his death at the age of 102. He was said to have a strong hatred of every kind of medicine and took some only once.

• • •

WHAT little is known of 'Scotch Meggy' was written up in *The Times* of 18 November 1834. As the nickname suggests, Meggy was Scottish. She was a strongly built woman, in her fifties and well known for her skillful rowing on the Thames. She had won several large wagers in this way. Scotch Meggy came to widespread public notice when she went to the aid of a policeman who was being beaten up by six men and a woman on Lambeth Street in London. Seeing the policeman being savagely attacked, 'she threw off her bonnet and shawl, and set to work in real earnest'. At the subsequent trial, the police praised her conduct. In answer to the magistrate's questions, Meggy said that she had spent forty-two years on board a man-of-war and had been present at several naval engagements. The Admiralty had rewarded her service with an annual pension of £25.

• • •

BELGIAN chess grandmaster George Koltanowski (1903–2000) set a new world record in Edinburgh on 20 September 1937 by playing thirty-four chess games simultaneously while blindfolded. The exhibition lasted for thirteen-and-a-half hours. Of the thirty-four matches, Koltanowski won twenty-four and drew ten. His record still stands in the *Guinness Book of Records*.

• • •

DAVID Lindsay, 1st Earl of Crawford (c.1366–1407) was a Scottish nobleman and a famed jousting champion. He fought the English champion Lord Welles during a tournament on 6 May 1390 and unhorsed his opponent so easily that the crowd began shouting that he had cheated by nailing himself to the saddle. To prove his innocence, Lindsay jumped off his horse and leapt back into the saddle while wearing a full suit of armour.

• • •

ON 6 August 1960, fifteen-year-old London schoolgirl Susan Baddeley achieved her goal of swimming the full length of Loch Lomond non-stop. It took twenty-nine hours and forty minutes for her to complete this arduous endeavour and she sang to keep herself awake. Her forty-seven-year-old father swam alongside her for company, and two boats carrying officials of the Long Distance Swimming Association and friends followed.

• • •

BASS Rock is a seven-acre island at the entrance of the Firth of Forth. It lies a little over a mile offshore and three miles from the nearest town of North Berwick. It is a steep-sided rocky outpost and once had a fort on it which was used as a jail centuries ago. Most famously, several Jacobite prisoners easily captured the fort with the aid of a garrison sergeant on 15 June 1691.

When the lieutenant-governor, a man called Wood, and some of the garrison were absent on the mainland and most of the remaining garrison were helping to unload a supply boat, the prisoners overpowered the remaining guards, shut the gates and turned the guns on those outside, forcing the military garrison to retreat to the mainland. The rebels were soon joined by other Jacobites from the mainland and managed to hold the island fortress for nearly three years.

The fortress was in a strong position high above the sea and easily defended. A poor blockade was launched against the handful of rebels, but they were easily resupplied with munitions and provisions and never suffered. They finally surrendered on 21 April 1694 and, with all the honours of war, were allowed to leave for France.

• • •

JOHN Brown (1722–87) from Carpow near Abernethy in Perthshire had little education yet a thirst for knowledge. Both his parents died when he was about twelve and Brown had to become a shepherd to support himself. In the following years he taught himself Greek, Latin, Hebrew, Arabic, Syriac, Persian, Ethiopian, French, Spanish, Dutch, German and Italian. He became a schoolmaster and later a clergyman.

•   •   •

ON 4 April 1993, Royal Navy divers retrieved a human liver from the wreckage of a light plane, in time to allow a transplant to occur that morning. The single-engined airplane, which was rushing the liver from Birmingham to Edinburgh, developed engine trouble around one o'clock in the morning and the pilot had to ditch in the mouth of the River Forth six miles east of Edinburgh. The pilot and co-pilot swam to shore and were later treated for shock. Divers retrieved the watertight case containing the liver in about twenty feet of water and rushed it to Edinburgh Royal Infirmary where the organ was successfully transplanted in a woman in her thirties.

•   •   •

A quick-thinking fireman, Brian Todd, was hailed as a hero in July 2005 for saving a goldfish's life. Todd and fellow workers had been called out to tackle a fire at Andrew Mouat's home in Liberton, Edinburgh. After the fire had been extinguished, Todd noticed that a goldfish in the house was barely alive. He resuscitated it by swirling it in water in the kitchen sink. Mouat, who was treated for smoke inhalation, was delighted that the firefighters had saved his pet.

•   •   •

SANDY Dobbie from Alloa, Clackmannanshire, set two new world records on 13 April 1999 when he cut the hair of twenty-three men in under an hour (fifty-nine minutes eighteen seconds) beating the old record of twenty-two haircuts in an hour. He also set a new record for the fastest haircut when he cut one man's hair in one minute, twenty seconds, beating the old record by almost a minute. Dobbie was a barber by profession and broke the records at Airth Castle, Falkirk, under *Guinness Book of Records* rules, to become the world's fastest barber.

• • •

PEEBLES-born William Douglas (1724–1810), 4th Duke of Queensberry, was one of the greatest gamblers of his era and famous for his unusual wagers. He once bet a considerable sum that he could send a letter fifty miles in one hour. The canny Duke won the bet by hiring twenty expert cricketers, who stood in a carefully measured circle and nimbly threw a cricket ball with the letter stuffed inside to one another. When the hour was up, it was discovered the letter had travelled many miles more than the distance to be covered by the wager.

On another occasion, Queensberry bet a Mr Pigot 500 guineas that Pigot's father would die before Sir William Codrington. Unknown to both men, Pigot's father had actually died on the morning of the day the wager was made. Neither man could have known this. Pigot refused to pay up, claiming that his father's death had occurred before the wager was made, and therefore it was void. Queensberry asserted that he had won the bet and he brought an action to the King's Bench for the money. The jury found in his favour.

In 1809, the old gambler made an even stranger bet. He wagered £500 that 'he would die at a certain hour on a certain date'. He lost the bet and paid up.

• • •

TWENTY-four Glasgow students claimed a new world record on 13 January 1960 by all cramming into a 1935 baby Austin car.

• • •

ALEXANDER McDonald (1771–c.1839) from Penrith was better known as Blind Alick to the people of Stirling. Blinded by smallpox as a child, McDonald was fortunate to be blessed with an excellent memory and was famed for reciting the Bible from memory. McDonald knew Stirling like the back of his hand and his senses were so acute that he could tell the colour of a person's coat by feeling it with his fingers. He made a living by busking as a fiddler during the day. In the evening his services were much in demand at social events.

• • •

AN anonymous Edinburgh man climbed a fifty-foot high Christmas tree in the city centre in December 2000 and changed the topmost bulb from white to red. He also left a note explaining that he had scaled the tree to prove his love for his girlfriend.

• • •

ON 30 August 1802 two men from Cumbernauld, Lanarkshire, wagered a considerable sum of money on a curious gamble. James Smith bet John Stobo that he could walk two miles backwards in under half an hour. To the surprise of many spectators, Smith performed the feat in exactly twenty minutes on the road between Glasgow and Falkirk in front of a large crowd that had gathered to witness the novel event.

• • •

IN the 1930s, an adventurous undergraduate at Aberdeen University climbed the spire of the 250-foot Mitchell Tower and tied a silk-hatted skeleton to the very tip. For over a week the skeleton was left there, to the amusement of the people of Aberdeen, before the figure was at last removed by a plucky steeplejack.

• • •

FATHER John Archie Macmillan once raised money to build a new community hall on the Hebridean island of Eriskay by playing the bagpipes while water-skiing.

• • •

ALEXANDER Drummond (1761–1857) from Stirling offered to enlist in the Seventy-ninth (Cameron) Highlanders in 1794 on condition that he would hold the rank of sergeant. To his surprise, his demand was complied with and he spent the next few years in the army, where he served with distinction. On his discharge, he returned to Stirling and 'fought his battles o'er again', recounting his many adventures to his friends old and new.

Natural Wonders

THOUSANDS of small frogs fell from the sky at Lanark Railway Station during a heavy downpour of rain on 7 August 1865. The shower lasted for five minutes and left the ground around the station thickly covered with small, hopping frogs. There were so many that witnesses were not able to avoid stepping on them, no matter how carefully they tried.

One person sent a description of the freak event to *The Scotsman* after reading about a similar frog fall in the Dumfries suburb of Maxwelltown on 17 August 1865. Around midday there was a heavy shower of rain, and at the junction of David Street and King Street it was particularly heavy. When the rain stopped, the ground was covered with thousands of small brown frogs 'about the size of an almond'. The ground was thickly covered with them along David Street, from the entrance to Palmerston Foundry to within fifty yards of Glasgow Street. The tiny frogs even choked street drains. Local children were delighted, scooped up handfuls of the frogs and carried them to pools of water to see them swimming.

• • •

WORKMEN were repairing the concrete pavement at Stumpy Corner, Girvan, Ayrshire, on 18 June 1932, when they unearthed several potatoes. Although small, the tubers were just like potatoes grown in open ground. The potatoes were discovered at a depth of two feet and the only solution to the mystery of how potatoes came to be thriving under concrete is that they may have spread from nearby Moot Hill, Knockcushan Gardens.

• • •

LIGHTNING flashes can leave shadow images of objects on exposed surfaces. In July 1892 a telephone company employee repairing a broken wire at a residence in Errol, Perthshire, discovered the picture of the roof of a neighbouring house on one of the white insulators. Lightning had probably flashed the picture on to the porcelain.

• • •

KIRBY'S Wonderful and Scientific Museum of 1820 contains accounts of two giant vegetables grown in Scotland. In 1811, James Cunningham from Kelso, Roxburghshire, grew a cabbage so enormous that its external leaves had a diameter of eighteen feet. The solid body of the plant was thirty-nine inches in circumference. In 1813, Colonel Burnet of Gudgirth, Ayrshire, grew a turnip that weighed twenty-four pounds, eight ounces and measured four feet, eleven inches in diameter.

• • •

LIGHTNING neatly cut a circle of glass from a windowpane in an Edinburgh house during a heavy thunderstorm on 8 June 1972. It happened around midday while the storm was passing overhead. No one was in the room. The lightning cut an almost circular hole, with dimensions of 4.9 cm by 4.6 cm. The cut out piece was found intact inside the room. Its edge and the edge of the glass surrounding the hole had a fused appearance and was smooth to touch on the inner side of the pane. An irregular crack ran across the pane from the bottom of the hole, and the window had broken along this crack.

• • •

THE largest tree to grow in Scotland was the remarkable great ash tree that once grew in the churchyard of Kilmalie in Lochaber, Inverness-shire. It burnt down in 1746, but its remains were not measured until 1764. At ground level its circumference was found to be fifty-eight feet.

• • •

AN extraordinary fall of oak leaves was witnessed in 1889 at Dalgonar Farm in the parish of Penpoint, Dumfriesshire, by a Mr Wright, who was out walking on the hills. His account was published in *Nature* in October 1890: 'I was struck by a strange appearance in the atmosphere, which I at first mistook for a flock of birds, but as I saw them falling to the earth my curiosity quickened. Fixing my eyes on one of the larger of them, and running about 100 yards up the hill until directly underneath, I awaited its arrival, when I found it to be an oak leaf. Looking upwards the air was thick with them, and as they descended in an almost vertical direction, oscillating, and glittering in the sunshine, the spectacle was as beautiful as rare. The wind was from the north, blowing a very gentle breeze, and there were occasional showers of rain. On examination of the hills after the leaves had fallen, it was found that they covered a tract of about a mile wide and two miles long. The leaves were wholly those of the oak. No oak leaves grow in clumps together nearer than eight miles.'

• • •

ON 9 June 1883, the image of a nearby yew tree was imprinted upon the body of a Berwickshire boy hurt by lightning. The image later faded away.

• • •

THE trunk of an old ash tree near Bonhill House in Dumbartonshire was measured four feet from the ground and found to have a circumference of thirty-four feet, one inch in September 1784. Its heart was decayed and the tree's owner, Sir Thomas Lauder, carved out a large room inside the tree and fitted it with glass windows and seating. The room's diameter was eight feet, five inches and its ceiling was eleven feet high. Eighteen people could comfortably dine inside the tree.

• • •

ALASTAIR Murray was driving down Jesmond Drive in Aberdeen on the afternoon of 8 September 1994 during heavy rain when a manhole cover shot out of the ground, lifting his Ford Escort about three feet in the air, damaging its chassis and sending the car flying thirty feet across the road on to a pavement. Murray was taken to hospital with back injuries. Police blamed a build-up of air pressure in the sewer after heavy rains, causing the manhole cover to explode.

• • •

ACCORDING to the *Symon's Monthly Meteorological Magazine* of September 1879, a rain of seaweed had fallen on the evening of 30 August on the Lomond Hills, near Falkirk. A heavy hailstorm, complete with thunder and lightning, had passed over the hills. The following morning 'the hills were found in several places to be covered with seaweed, or some substance as nearly resembling it as possible, and it was also seen hanging from the trees and shrubberies in the district. In some places the weed lay in a pretty thick coating, so that quantities of it could be collected from the grass'. The Lomond Hills lie some ten miles from the Firth of Forth.

• • •

ON 13 August 1849, immediately after a loud peel of thunder, a thick block of ice twenty feet in circumference fell on the estate of one Mr Moffat of Ballullich, near Ord on the Isle of Skye. The ice was almost entirely transparent and composed of square and diamond-shaped crystals from one to three inches in length. No other hail or snow was visible.

• • •

A remarkable multiple mirage was observed on 5 December 1922 by light-keeper John Anderson at Cape Wrath Lighthouse in Sutherland. Around 10.30 am, Anderson was observing some sheep grazing on a hill about a quarter of a mile away to the south through his telescope when he noticed an unusual mirage replicating the coastline from Cape Wrath to Dunnet Head. The mirage was a perfect copy of what would be seen from a distance of about ten miles out to sea and the image was replicated three times. In other words, to the south of the lighthouse there were three repetitions of the mirage one above the other, with the sea separating each image. Landmarks could be distinguished in the mirages. Anderson said the mirage was not visible to the naked eye and could be seen only through a telescope from a particular vantage-point.

• • •

A phosphorescent tree was discovered in a wood on the Cleland estate in Wishaw, Lanarkshire, in August 1908. Some young men were out at night in the woods when they were startled by what they thought was a ghost. Approaching it, they discovered it was a glowing ash tree, the trunk of which gave out so strong a light, it was good enough to read by.

• • •

ON 24 July 1818, a strange fall of ice occurred on the island of Stronsay in the Orkneys. Giant hailstones of many varieties rained down on part of the island and within ten minutes caused havoc, destroying crops, wounding animals and breaking windows. On one farm the hailstones were said to have lain one-and-a-half feet deep on the ground and all around looked like fields of ice. Some of the hail was round 'like eggs', but most were flat and jagged and had a greyish-white colour. The largest hailstones measured six inches in circumference. The hail fell with such force that it was driven into the earth to a depth of four inches. It killed countless numbers of birds. After an hour, most of the hailstones had melted away, leaving a strong sulphurous smell lingering in their wake.

•   •   •

THERE are many recorded occurrences of showers of fish in Scotland over the past two centuries. For example, on 21 April 1828, Major Forbes Mackenzie from Fodderty in Strathpeffer, Ross, was crossing a field on his farm when he saw that a large part of it was covered with herring fry of between three and four inches long. The fish were fresh and intact. Major Mackenzie's farm lay three miles from the sea.

On 3 March 1830, the inhabitants of the island of Islay in the Hebrides were surprised to find large numbers of small herrings scattered all over their fields after a day of heavy rain. Some of the fish were still alive.

On 13 June 1832, a shower of small herrings fell near Castlehill in Argyllshire. The largest of these were about two inches long, but most were described as being 'about the size of small minnows'. Castlehill lies about four miles from the sea.

•   •   •

ON 28 November 1888, hailstones shaped like pyramids (with four flat sides and a convex base) fell near Edinburgh. The hailstones were transparent, but had numerous water-filled cavities.

• • •

THE largest recorded meteorite to land in Scotland fell near Strathmore, Tayside, on 3 December 1917. It weighed 10.09 kilograms and was the largest of four stones that fell (total weight 13.3 kilograms).

Ingenious Inventions

VOLUME II of Sir Walter Scott's book *Border Antiquities* (1814) describes the iron hand of the Clephanes of Carslogie. This hand is said to have been made on the orders of Robert the Bruce and was gifted to his faithful follower, Allan de Clephane of Carslogie, who had lost his left hand at the battle of Bannockburn. Its clever design allowed Clephane to easily open and close the fingers, thus allowing him to hold a horse's reins.

• • •

IN January 1972, it was back to the drawing board for John Andrew of Glasgow, who thought he had created a brilliant way to cut down on his electricity bill. Sixty-one-year-old Andrew mounted a fan on his car roof and another on a side mirror. When the car was in motion, the fans charged batteries in the car boot. Andrew claimed that a 100-mile drive produced thirty hours of electricity for his home.

Unfortunately, not everybody appreciated his invention and Andrew found himself in court because the fan on the side mirror was deemed to be a potential danger to other drivers. The judge had no problem with the roof-mounted fan and complimented Andrew for his ingenuity, but fined him £95 for the hazard the one on his side mirror had posed.

• • •

IN 1969, a Glasgow businessman customised his car by covering it with 'fur' to advertise his business. To touch, the 'fur' was described as feeling like the nap of a snooker table. The effect was achieved by painting the car with an epoxy resin. Then it was coated with the 'fur' – man made fibres – by means of an electrical current. The car's owner, R.B. Whitehead, ran a company that provided this kind of finish for the interior walls of hotels and bars. When he parked his car, Whitehead left a sign in the window which read: 'You can touch it. It won't bite.'

• • •

G.L.O. Davidson from Banchory, Aberdeenshire, spent a lot of time and money trying to invent a vertical take-off, passenger-carrying machine. By late 1907, he was in Denver, Colorado, working on his latest design, an enormous flying machine with a pair of 120-blade rotary 'lifters'. On 8 May 1908, Davidson decided to test his flying machine with himself as the pilot. He nervously turned the boiler of the inadequate Stanley steam engine up to 600-800 pounds (272–363 kilograms) of pressure. The machine briefly lifted off the ground before the top blew off the boiler. According to the aviation historian Philip Jarrett, Davidson was undeterred by his machine's failure and returned to Britain to set about building another improved flying machine, but it was never completed.

• • •

IN the 1860s it was revealed that a Scottish gentleman had trained a couple of mice and invented machinery for them to spin yarn using a treadmill. The article says that the apparatus was constructed for the mice to 'make atonement to society for past offences by twisting and reeling from 100 to 200 threads per day. To complete this, the little pedestrian has to run ten and a half miles. This journey it performs every day with ease.' It goes on to describe in depth plans to upscale and commercialise the mouse-mill machinery a thousand fold. The entire story sounds like a hoax, but at least it is an entertaining and original one.

• • •

IN 1934, the General Post Office was looking into ways of improving the postal service to remote Scottish islands when young German scientist Gerhard Zucker proposed a novel solution to the problem. He suggested using a rocket to carry post (and eventually medical supplies) between the islands. With official support, Zucker was given permission to demonstrate the viability of his idea.

The tiny island of Scarp, half a mile off the Isle of Harris, was selected as the location of the first over-sea test of a letter-carrying rocket. Some 1,200 letters addressed to friends, relatives and dignitaries were packed into a metre-long rocket that was to be fired across the stretch of sea to Harris, where the rocket would be unloaded and delivered to the nearest post office. Attached to the letters were special stamps issued to commemorate the occasion.

The trial took place on 28 July 1934, but did not go according to plan. The rocket exploded, scattering the letters like confetti over the beach at Scarp. Undaunted by this setback, Zucker made another attempt two days later – with the same spectacular and unsuccessful result.

• • •

GEORGE Bennie (1891–1957) from Glasgow designed and built the Bennie Railplane, a futuristic monorail train that he believed would carry passengers at high speeds in comfort, above existing rail lines carrying slower-moving freight. In 1929 a quarter-of-a-mile test track was built 30 foot over an existing railway line at Milngavie, on the outskirts of Glasgow.

The Bennie Railplane was a streamlined cigar-shaped carriage driven by aircraft propellers at each end. It was suspended from a single overhead rail, but a stabilising rail underneath prevented the carriage from swaying. Many successful demonstrations were made, but Bennie was unable to attract investors and his brilliant invention was ultimately scrapped.

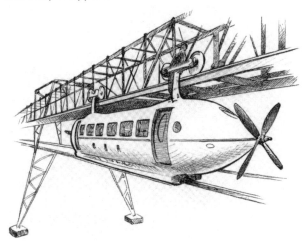

Extreme Measures

IN the early 1960s, the *RMS Victoria* was the largest bolt-assembled vessel ever built in one country for re-erection in another. It was first built at the shipyard of Yarrow & Co. Ltd. in Glasgow and then disassembled in order to be shipped to its buyers in Africa. The ship was ordered in the late 1950s when it was realised that two steamers were not sufficient to meet the shipping needs on Lake Victoria. The mail-order vessel was shipped out to Africa in 1960 in 1,200 crates weighing in all about 1,200 tons. It was reassembled in the Kenyan lake port of Kisumu under the direction of a team from Yarrow. When completed, it became a 261–foot vessel of 1,570 gross-tonnage and successfully carried freight and people across Lake Victoria for many years.

• • •

ON 25 February 1948, twenty-three-year-old Robert Carvil from Glasgow, who swam across the Clyde at night in a blinding snowstorm to win a bet, was fined £2 for a breach of the peace. The amount Carvil won was said to be considerably more than his fine.

• • •

IN May 2003, a sailor serving in the Gulf War returned home to Edinburgh to find that a neighbour had started legal proceedings against him because he had not contributed to the cost of mowing a communal lawn during his eighty-six days at sea. Robert Williamson, from Davidson's Mains, was at sea when his neighbour started legal action to force him to pay the £46.88 bill he had forgotten about.

• • •

ON 11 January 1928, a Scotsman appeared at Liverpool Police Court with his head swathed in bandages.

'That is all show,' said an Irishman who was charged with hitting the Scotsman with a kettle. 'He was walking about without bandages yesterday.'

When the magistrate asked him if this was true, the Scotsman said it was, explaining that he wanted to keep the bandages clean for his court appearance.

• • •

WEALTHY Glasgow car enthusiast eighty-six-year-old Albert Rickard filled out his twelfth application for a driving test on 24 January 1961. Rickard owned eight cars but after he had been involved in an accident in 1960, a court suspended his licence until he had passed a driving test. After failing his eleventh test on 23 January, Rickard said, 'I think some licence testers would be out of a job if they didn't have me around.'

• • •

IN July 1967, a Scotsman and a Frenchman got into an argument over a girl and agreed that the only way to settle their dispute was by a duel with rapiers. The Scotsman, Daniel Allan, drew first blood – his own, when he cut his hand while breaking into a museum in Blantyre, Lanarkshire, to steal two swords. He was spotted by a policeman, arrested and later fined. The Frenchman – Allan did not know his name – escaped.

• • •

A hard-boiled egg carefully wrapped in tissue paper was deposited in a Glasgow bank in February 1964. According to the manager, it was a perfectly good cheque worth thirteen guineas. A Glasgow businessman had been dining out with friends and realised when he went to pay the bill that he had left his wallet and chequebook at home. He ordered a hard-boiled egg and wrote a cheque for the amount of the bill on its shell and signed it.

• • •

THE tragedy of an Aberdeen family who were too proud to accept charity from neighbours came to light on 15 May 1935 when police broke in to their house and discovered the almost mummified bodies of an elderly man and his sister. Another sister lay on a plank bed in a poor condition; she was barely able to speak. Police had been alerted when neighbours realised that nobody had seen the reclusive family, who lived in 10 King Street, in a long time. On searching the house, the police discovered £90 in a cupboard, which the surviving sixty-three-year-old woman explained the family were afraid to spend on food for fear they would be unable to pay the rent.

She could not remember when she had last eaten and thought her brother and sister were only sleeping, begging the police not to disturb them. A post mortem revealed that sixty-one-year-old Frederick Sutcliffe Summers and his seventy-one-year-old sister had been dead for at least two months. At one time, the family had been well-to-do, but had then been reduced to poverty. Neighbours said that Summers had not been seen outdoors since he had failed to pass his final law exam at Aberdeen University. Following this disappointment, Summers had taken to his bed and remained there for more than 40 years, tended by his sisters.

• • •

IN 1794, Jane, 4th Duchess of Gordon, famously helped recruit soldiers for the newly formed Gordon Highlanders regiment in an unusual way. She wore a military uniform and a large black, feathered hat and travelled to Scotland to recruit men. She placed each recruit's enlistment shilling between her lips and allowed the men to collect it by kissing her.

• • •

THE body of Scotsman Donald McDonald was exhumed from a graveyard in Sydney, Australia, on 22 January 1953, but the coffin did not contain the wooden leg in which his relatives believed he had hidden his fortune, inside a secret compartment. The fifty-three-year-old retired seaman was penniless when he died in April 1951, but his relatives on the Isle of Mull thought otherwise and asked for the exhumation.

• • •

TWO middle-aged men dropped dead in Inverness in December 1974 within minutes of each other after a contest to see who could drink a half bottle of whisky more quickly.

• • •

A Glasgow doctor, who died at the end of the nineteenth century, had been deserted by his wife and so left his estate to his sisters. In his will, however, he asked his sister Elizabeth to provide his former spouse with 'a gift of ten shillings sterling, to buy her a pocket handkerchief to weep after my decease'.

• • •

A hoax in aid of Greenock hospital fooled thousands of people in September 1933. The hoaxers inserted a brief article in a Port Glasgow newspaper announcing that Miss F.N. Tynne and her mechanic Mr L.S. Dee had flown from Vancouver, Canada, across the Atlantic on a secret record-breaking attempt, but they had crash-landed near Port Glasgow. The article said Miss Tynne would make a public announcement about the flight at Greenock Central Station on the evening of 28 September.

Despite the aviators' odd names, the public lapped up the

story. Some people even rang up the Greenock hospital to enquire about how Miss Tynne was getting on. The police had to field numerous calls and despite doing their best to explain that the story was a prank perpetrated by students to raise money for a hospital, the hoax gained widespread credibility. Souvenir hunters set off in search of the wreck and the national press picked up the story. Some newspapers were fooled into including updates about the 'air disaster' at Port Glasgow.

The students were delighted at the enormous publicity they had created. Thousands of people turned up to meet the 'Canadian' aviators at Greenock and the students were on hand to collect money for the hospital. Two students dressed as aviators were paraded through the streets.

• • •

PRINCESS Margaret was born at Glamis Castle in Angus on 21 August 1930. The registration of her birth was delayed so that her number on the register would not be the unlucky number thirteen.

• • •

GLASGOW man Harry Hamilton was fishing one day in September 1966, but the trout were ignoring his live bait. Frustrated by his failure to land a single fish, Hamilton resorted to desperate measures. He clipped off several strands of his long brown moustache and made an artificial fly. On his fourth cast with this novel bait, he landed a one-and-a-half pound trout.

• • •

ON 1 October 1843, a blacksmith named Thomson entered the Secession Church, Main Street, Glasgow, where St George's Free Congregation was gathered for worship. Thomson climbed into the pulpit, calmly poured a glass of whisky and proposed a toast to 'The Crown and the Congregation'. When Thomson tried to make a quick exit, two of the shocked congregation seized him and the police were called. Thomson was fined £10 or sixty days in jail and freely admitted that his outrageous actions had been carried out for a bet of five shillings.

• • •

A curious court case was heard in Dundee in May 1876. When Councillor Blair visited a house in Hilltown, seven 'married wives, who had gathered on the landing of the stairs, enjoyed a joke at his expense by tying the door with a rope to the stair railing, thus imprisoning him for some time'. Blair did not see the funny side of the prank and brought the women to court. In her defence, the house's owner, Mrs Pepper, said she had done it because she was tired of Mr Blair's frequent visits to her home. Mrs Pepper was fined fifteen shillings or sentenced to five days in prison if she did not pay.

• • •

ON 31 March 1972, a team of zoologists from Flamingo Park Zoo in Yorkshire were at Loch Ness searching for proof of the famous monster's existence when they discovered a mysterious carcass floating in the lake. Reports claimed that it weighed a ton and a half and was fifteen-and-a-half feet long. Some witnesses described the creature as having a bear's head and a brown scaly body, with claw-like flippers. Others said it had a green body with no scales and looked like a cross between a walrus and a seal.

The excited zoologists loaded up their mysterious find and were driving back to the zoo with it when they were stopped by Scottish police acting under a 1933 act of parliament which prohibited the removal of 'unidentified creatures' from Loch Ness. The body was then taken to Dunfermline for identification in the glare of the world media. Edinburgh scientists quickly identified the creature as a bull elephant seal, native to the South Atlantic.

The following day, April Fool's Day, Flamingo Park's education officer, John Shields, confessed that he had been responsible for the hoax. The previous week a bull elephant seal had died at Dudley Zoo and he decided to use the body to play a prank on his monster-hunting colleagues – never imagining his hoax would get so much media attention. Shields had shaved off the dead animal's whiskers, stuffed its cheeks with stones and frozen it for several days before depositing it into Loch Ness, making sure his colleagues would find it.

• • •

IN May 1961, when word got around that dealer Alexander Little had dumped a large number of old televisions in a lake near the mining village of Cronberry in Ayrshire, locals went fishing for them. The miners fished quite a number of televisions from the water, dried them out and were delighted to discover that most of them worked perfectly.

• • •

WHEN John B. Henderson, the chess correspondent of *The Scotsman*, landed in Seattle in April 2001 at the height of a foot and mouth crisis, US customs officers confiscated his haggis. They took it out onto the runway and shot it five times before dowsing it with petrol.

• • •

SAMMY Maxwell learned the hard way not to invade a tiger's cage. The nine-year-old collected bird's eggs and nearly died for his hobby on 28 June 1959 in a tiger's cage at Glasgow Zoo. Sammy spotted a nest under the eaves of a roof in the tiger's enclosure. Not seeing the animal around, the boy jumped a guard rail and started to climb the cage bars to get inside and check the nest. The Malayan tiger, described as 'savage' by his keeper, chose this moment to return to the cage from an adjoining one. He saw the boy climbing the bars and jumped at him, ripping Sammy's leather jacket.

• • •

GAVIN Shanks saved his pot-bellied pig in June 1998 by giving it the kiss of life. Shanks was showing a customer around his farm near Carluke, Lanarkshire, when he saw his pet pig Tam floating face down in his swimming pool. Shanks jumped in fully clothed and pulled the pig out of the water. Seeing that Tam was not breathing, Shanks began giving him heart massage and then the kiss of life to get air into his lungs. 'I thought we'd lost him,' said Shanks, 'but he gave a little cough just as I was giving up, so I kept going. He seems to be back to normal. He's running about the farmyard quite the thing now.'

• • •

IN 1942, six-year-old Robbie Wilson got bored at his sister Edna's fourth birthday party and ran out to play in the street outside his Edinburgh home. A passing driver swerved but hit the child, killing him. The driver carried the boy into the house and then collapsed. A doctor treated the boy's parents and the motorist for shock. Then the man left. He did not tell the Wilsons his name and they knew only that he lived in Sunderland in England.

A year later, on Edna's next birthday, a large parcel arrived for the girl. Inside was a large rocking horse. There was no sender's name and the only clue to its origin was the postmark: Sunderland. For years Edna received expensive birthday presents from the man. When she married in October 1961, he sent a wedding present, leaving the family to wonder how the Sunderland man had found out that Edna was getting married.

• • •

WHEN Glasgow man William Reid died in September 1960, he left a set of unusual instructions in his will for his executor: 'This may come to you as a great surprise, to be able to count the miser's hoard. This is what I want you to do: Get the case out of the cupboard with "C.R." on it. The key can be found in a tin with beans in it. This case contains all the things you require – policies, title deeds, insurance, record cards etc . . . Collect the old case from the sideboard. There is a cash box in it. There is also a cash box at the bottom of the kitchen cupboard with a few cans on top of it. There is a pocket book between the two mattresses and another below the centre lump of coal at the back of the bunker. In the old clock on the top shelf there are a few pounds. Make sure you find everything.' The executor did. It amounted to £2,518.

• • •

AN Irishman served as a proxy bridegroom in Kansas City on 26 May 1944 when a Scotsman (who was thousands of miles away in Glasgow) was married to an American woman in a specially arranged legally binding ceremony. Marjorie Snowden from Media, Pennsylvania, became the bride of Richard Rolls Murray from Glasgow, with her brother-in-law, Belfast-born William Porter, standing in as the proxy groom.

Crazy Creatures

THE Laing Museum in the small town of Newburgh, Fife, preserves the stuffed body of a two-headed kitten born in the nineteenth century on nearby Mugdrum Island.

• • •

AN Airedale belonging to Elgin, Morayshire, tobacconist Sinclair Hunter had a charmed life. By the age of fourteen months, in May 1929, it had been run over by a car and hit by a bus, but had escaped unharmed each time. Later the dog escaped from an attic room by climbing out onto the roof and jumping twenty-seven feet onto one of Elgin's busiest streets. It landed unhurt and successfully tracked down its master.

• • •

IN November 2006, fate played a cruel trick on a rare visitor to Britain. A red-rumped swallow (*Hirundo daurica*) from southern Europe took a wrong turn on its annual migration to Africa and ended up in Lunan Bay near Montrose in Angus. Normally the rare swallow was not found any farther north than Greece and its arrival delighted bird watchers, who flocked to the area to see the welcome visitor. As they looked on in horror, a Scottish sparrow hawk swooped down and killed the swallow. The species only occasionally turned up in Britain during its migration season. A specimen had previously been seen in the Tayside area in 1987.

• • •

TIKI the monkey was banished to a zoo by his owner in June 1962 because he was becoming an alcoholic. 'I bought him from a man about a month ago,' said Findlay Sinclair, who ran the Red Lion Hotel in Culross, Fife. 'I thought he would amuse the customers in the bar, but he didn't. He began drinking the customers' beer. Then he got on the hard stuff – whisky. In fact, he was well on his way to becoming an alcoholic.'

• • •

IN September 1890, a cat gave birth to four kittens at a house in Haddington, East Lothian, and set up home in a summerhouse in the garden. The owner later removed three of the kittens. When the owner visited the summerhouse the following day, she was surprised to see that the last kitten had also disappeared. A search was made, but the kitten could not be found. Over the next few days the mother cat's movements were monitored and she was spotted repeatedly going to a thick honeysuckle bush in the garden. The missing kitten was found safely tucked away in a blackbird's nest seven feet off the ground in the thickest part of the honeysuckle.

• • •

A Belted Galloway cow survived an eighty-foot fall from a cliff at Muchalls, Aberdeenshire on 26 April 2000, when she missed rocks and landed on a patch of grass.

• • •

IN July 1997, staff at the Oban Sea Life Centre in Argyllshire put a plastic owl named McDougal on display to scare away seagulls who were stealing food out of the mouths of two pregnant seals. The birds would swoop down on the two seals, Blonde and Gigha, and make off with their fish. McDougal was donated by a local hardware store of the same name.

• • •

A dog (presumably accidentally) shot and killed another dog in a freak occurrence on 31 May 1944. A Perthshire gamekeeper described the tragic event to *The Times*. He had been on the Auchlyne grouse moor hunting vermin. From his hiding place on the top of a hill, he had shot a fox at the bottom of a nearby cliff. He climbed down to retrieve it, carrying a dog under his arm, but leaving behind his gun and another dog on the summit. Suddenly a shot rang out and the dog in the keeper's arms was hit and killed. The gamekeeper was unhurt. It was later found that the dog left with the gun had stepped on the trigger.

• • •

TWO horses saved a baby that had been deserted by its mother in a wood near Aberdeen in June 1928. One night the woman placed her sixteen-day-old son at the foot of a tree in a dense forestry plantation. Its only covering was a shawl. The following afternoon a farmer was working near the plantation with a pair of horses. Every time they got close to the plantation, they stopped and had to be urged on. Finally, they refused to move. The farmer's wife and two men entered the wood and found the baby. Though blue with cold, it was alive and crying faintly. Its mother was traced and sentenced to three months' jail for abandoning her infant son and endangering his life.

• • •

AT the Clyde naval base at Faslane, Argyllshire, in July 2008, sailors looked on in astonishment as a seagull swooped down and snatched a five-week-old kitten from its mother. The kitten struggled free and fell on to the razor sharp barbed wire surrounding the base. She was rescued and taken to a local vet to have her wounds stitched up.

• • •

THE *New York Times* of 27 June 1888 copied a report from the London *Pall Mall Gazette* applauding a Scottish collie's tenacious homing ability. A Coatbridge man sent a collie as a present to a friend in Buncrana, Co. Donegal in Ireland via the Glasgow to Londonderry ferry. His friend later sent a letter thanking him for the dog. A day or two later a telegram came saying that the collie had disappeared. Soon afterwards the collie showed up in the Coatbridge man's shop. He immediately sent the dog back to Donegal on a steamer.

Soon after he arrived in Buncrana, the dog again fled and returned to his old home in Lanarkshire.

• • •

THE most specialized feeder among birds in Britain and Ireland is the Scottish Crossbill (*Loxia Scotica*). Its bill is one of the most efficient natural tools in the world, enabling the bird to crack apart conifer cones in order to eat their seeds.

• • •

KYLE the cat used up at least one of his nine lives when he got trapped in the rafters of a garage roof for seven weeks in late 2002 without food or water. Kyle's owner, Edinburgh woman Judith Auld, had left the three-year-old cat with her mother in Dollar, Clackmannanshire, while her family headed off for a holiday in late July. When they returned, the cat had gone missing. The family gave Kyle up for lost after several weeks of searching around the area and putting appeals in the local paper.

When Auld heard that a cat fitting Kyle's description had been rescued from a garage roof near her mother's, she was delighted. 'I went along to the vets to see if it was Kyle and I hardly recognised him, although he knew me at once. He was a shadow of his former self.' Vet Kenny Laing was amazed Kyle had survived so long. Trapped by his neck in the garage's rafters, the cat had survived by licking condensation on the underside of the galvanized roof.

• • •

IN May 2006, a lifeboat crew was dispatched to rescue a young deer, which was spotted swimming out to sea from Arbroath harbour in Angus. By the time the crew reached it, the animal was exhausted from its attempts to climb up on the other harbour wall. 'It was trapped and in a very bad way – very distressed,' lifeboat man Allan Russell said. 'It was virtually dead when we came up alongside it.' Animal welfare experts said the deer must have been frightened by something and took to the water to escape. After it had made a full recovery, it was released on farmland.

• • •

BLACKIE Boy, a four-year-old pet Pekinese belonging to Mr and Mrs David Beattie from Ceres, Fife, featured in newspapers around the world in January 1950 when it became public knowledge that he was a talking dog. According to Mrs Beattie, Blackie Boy could repeat four phrases and had been talking since he was eighteen months old. The dog could say 'Hello', 'No, no, not now', 'Yum yum' and 'Fifi'. Fifi was the Beatties' other Pekinese; she could not talk. Mrs Beattie said that Blackie Boy occasionally spoke a few words at dog shows and once a fellow exhibitor fainted after hearing him talk. W.J. Rice, a veterinary surgeon, listened to Blackie Boy and described the dog's speech as 'pure mimicry of his mistress' voice', saying that his abilities were just like those of a talking budgerigar.

• • •

A tiny rare owl was saved in June 2004 after it was found stranded on an oil rig 110 miles off the coast of Aberdeen.

Experts said that the rare Scops owl from southern Europe had been sighted in Scotland only a few times before. The seven-inch owl was found in an exhausted state on the Fortress Delta platform. It was taken by helicopter to the Grampian Wildlife Rehabilitation Trust's wildlife hospital in New Deer, Aberdeenshire, and was released back into the wild on 9 June.

The owl had landed on the rig after being blown off course by heavy winds. If it had not found the rig, it would have died. The bird was worn out by its struggle and had lost ten percent of its body weight. Special care was taken of this rare visitor and it was nursed back to health by feeding it small bits of cut-up rabbit.

• • •

JAMES Johnson from Reawick in the Shetland Islands was out sailing his boat off Skelda Ness on 3 April 1935 with only his dog for company. A sudden squall capsized the boat as the sixty-six-year-old was heading for home and both man and dog ended up in the water. The boat was sinking fast, sucking Johnson down with it, but the faithful dog seized Johnson's clothing in its teeth and held him up until he could grab hold of an oar. Luckily for the pair, the accident had been seen and a boat had already put out to rescue them from the icy waters.

• • •

AN eagle was saved by Glasgow ornithologist Douglas Weir in April 1968 when he found the bird after it had lost one of its legs in a trap. He had a veterinary surgeon make and fit a new one out of a light alloy.

• • •

CUSTOMERS in a vegetable shop in Inverness fled on 2 March 1954 when a cow fell through the ceiling. The animal had escaped a nearby cattle market and had climbed a flight of stairs adjoining the shop to evade a pursuer, only to have the landing collapse under her weight.

• • •

IN February 2005 Marilyn King of Cumbernauld, near Glasgow, was worried when her recently purchased thirteen-year-old parrot, Nelson, started wheezing. He developed a terrible cough, and would groan and repeatedly call for help. A vet examined the ailing parrot but could find nothing wrong with him. The mystery was solved when Marilyn learned that Nelson had once lived in a nursing home and was copying the sounds he had heard there. He was an expert at groaning, as if he was getting out of a chair, and he sang like an old man. The parrot also muttered unintelligibly to himself and cried for help a lot. 'He has a whole repertoire of coughs,' Marilyn said, 'but his smoker's cough is the best.'

• • •

JOHN and Edna Jenkins from Penicuik, Midlothian, were saved from a fire by their cat in December 1997. The couple were fast asleep when a fire started in their garden hut and began to spread to the garage adjoining the house, putting them at risk. John had taught their tomcat Micha to ring a battery-powered bell whenever he wanted to go outside.

When the cat became aware of the fire, it kept ringing the bell and eventually woke up John. He got up, saw the rising flames and dialled 999 for the fire brigade. John had enough time to move his car out of danger and pull a potentially lethal gas cylinder from the garage out of the fire's path. 'I'm glad Micha was up to the tricks I've taught him,' he later remarked. 'He's been well fed on fresh haddock ever since that night.'

●　●　●

THOUSANDS of jellyfish were sucked into and clogged a coolant water intake, causing authorities to shut down the nuclear power station at Hunterston, Ayrshire, in August 1991.

●　●　●

A letter in *The Scotsman* on 20 July 1949 was from a reader from Keills, Argyllshire, who had spotted something unusual a few days before. While inspecting the famous Celtic cross at Keills Chapel, he saw two entangled birds fluttering about the hillside. They seemed to be in difficulty, so he tried to help them. He managed to catch the two stonechats and was amazed to discover that they were Siamese twins. The two young birds were joined together with a cord about the thickness of a lead pencil, just at the base of their wings. The birds were otherwise perfectly normal and healthy.

●　●　●

IN August 2008, Chris Morrison from Dunfermline noticed that his black Labrador Retriever, Oscar, rattled when he walked. He took him to a veterinarian to be checked out after feeling his dog's stomach and hearing something rattling around inside. Rosyth veterinarian Bob Hesketh operated on Oscar. During the hour-long operation, he removed thirteen golf balls from the five-year-old dog's stomach.

'It was like a magic trick. I opened him up and felt what I thought were two or three golf balls. But they just kept coming until we had a bagful,' Hesketh explained in wonder. The balls must have been in Oscar's stomach for months. Morrison explained that he usually took Oscar for a walk on a golf course near his home and the dog frequently hunted for lost balls around the ninth and twelfth fairways. Oscar recovered well from his operation and now wears a muzzle during his walk on the golf course.

• • •

DUNCAN Whyte was working in a warehouse at Bowmore Distillery in Linlithgow in May 1993. He had gone outside on an errand when colleagues heard him yell and saw Whyte stagger back into the warehouse holding his head in pain. Outside the building lay a full-grown swan. The unfortunate bird had flown into overhead wires, bounced off the warehouse roof and crashed on to Whyte's head. The warehouse worker was sore, but otherwise unhurt, while the swan had been killed by the multiple impacts.

• • •

POLICE rushed to a home after an emergency call was made on 31 August 2000 from a house in Kelty, Fife. They were alerted by an emergency line operator who was concerned that the caller may have collapsed or been unable to talk, since all she could hear was a dog barking. When police arrived at the house they found that it was unoccupied except for an 'agitated' dog standing next to an upset telephone. It appeared that the dog had knocked over the phone and accidentally dialled 999. A police spokesperson said: 'We are pleased to have collared the culprit and are putting this one down to experience, as a false alarm with good intent.'

• • •

PIGEONS outwitted their would-be captors in Leven, Fife, in March 1951. A large flock, some 200 strong, had been making a nuisance of themselves by perching on the town hall, and the Leven town council decided to try to capture them. The pigeons were fed a large amount of grain soaked in whisky – the council's ploy was to get the birds drunk and so catch them more easily. The pigeons happily tucked into their boozy meal, 'then soared drunkenly back to their rooftops and teetered there until they sobered up', as one newspaper put it. Instead of dealing with the avian menace once and for all, the council had merely thrown them a party. Borough Surveyor A.V. Samuel, who had dreamed up the plan, was quoted as saying, 'Either the whisky is watered down these days or these birds are old drinking hands.'

• • •

ON 22 July 1997, a python belonging to an Aberdeen man, Joss Clark, escaped from its owner during a descaling session. It appeared in his neighbour's toilet bowl two floors down. In panic, she flushed the toilet but the snake was retrieved unharmed. A few days later a four-foot boa constrictor slithered out of a waste tank at Nigg Head sewage works.

• • •

NEWS that Rusty, a blind German shepherd dog, and his collie guide dog needed a new home brought a flood of offers from across Britain in April 1954. Their owner, Dudley Stilton, was forced to place them in a kennel after moving from his house in England to rooms in Glasgow. When he said he could not afford to keep the two dogs in a kennel and would have to have them destroyed unless someone provided a home for them, the story was published in the national press and an avalanche of offers followed: 'My wife and I are overwhelmed,' Stilton said. 'The problem now is which offer to accept.' He had bought the collie two years before and had trained him to escort Rusty by an attached collar after the German shepherd had lost his sight in a meningitis attack.

• • •

A ewe belonging to Andrew Gibbs, Brockloch, New Cumnock, Ayrshire, gave birth to an extraordinary freak of nature on 27 April 1933. It had three eyes, two normal and one between them. The lamb had two noses, two tongues, but only one mouth. It also had four horns, two on top of the head and one on each side.

• • •

OLGA Fraser from Colinton, Edinburgh, was entertaining some friends in January 2003 when she noticed that the butter knife had vanished. She realised that her fourteen-year-old Golden Labrador had swallowed the knife. Waldo, a retired guide dog, had a well-earned reputation as a bit of a thief. He had jumped up to steal some butter from the dining table and had managed to swallow the table knife at the same time. Olga immediately brought Waldo to her local vet, Donald Mactaggart.

Within two hours of him swallowing the knife, Waldo was operated on after the knife was located in his gullet. 'I couldn't believe my eyes when I saw the X-ray,' Olga recalled. The knife had a six-inch blade and was in a precarious position inside Waldo. 'Thankfully, the knife wasn't sharp or serrated and the butter acted as a lubricant, so it slowly slipped down his gullet to his stomach,' Mactaggart recalled. 'It was quite a delicate operation because any slip may have damaged his gullet and because it was so close to his heart.'

Waldo was well on the way to recovery and was in 'splendid form' when Olga was interviewed by a newspaper. 'I don't know if he'll ever go near the butter again,' she added.

• • •

WHEN Louise Duguid and her brother Graeme found that their two-year-old pet hamster, Hector, was cold and lifeless at their home in Gifford, Lothian, in January 1992, they put him inside a cardboard box and buried him about a foot underground in their garden. Two hours later, a neighbour called to say that Hector was running about her garden! He had revived in the warmth of the box and dug himself out of his grave. The children, whose father was a pet insurance salesman, thereafter called Hector 'Lazarus'.

• • •

ON 9 January 1931, a gamekeeper and a friend were walking across lands at Cape Wrath in Sutherland when a golden eagle suddenly swooped down and flew off carrying a struggling stoat in its claws. The eagle flew high into the air, then began to fall with a corkscrew motion and crashed to the ground near the two men. To their astonishment, the stoat ran out from beneath the bird and quickly disappeared. They picked up the eagle and saw that it had died from a large wound in its neck. It had been killed by its intended prey, the stoat, who turned the tables on its attacker – in mid-air!

• • •

A dog survived for three weeks trapped on a ledge at Carradale, Argyllshire, before being rescued. The Stewart family, from Eckford, Roxburghshire, had been holidaying in the area when their border terrier Daisy went missing on 12 October 2006. After a long search and poster campaign had come to nothing, the Stewarts had given up hope of finding her.

Then they had welcome news. On 29 October the 18-month-old dog was found trapped on a cliff ledge twenty feet above the sea by two divers who had heard her barking. Daisy must have fallen over the cliff edge, but survived by drinking rainwater. The Stewart family were delighted to be reunited with their much-loved pet.

• • •

ACCORDING to the *Guinness Book of Records* of 1996, the most prolific mouse catcher of all time was Towser, a female tortoiseshell cat, resident at the Famous Grouse Glenturret Whisky Distillery at Crieff in Perthshire. Born in April 1963, Towser caught an incredible total of 28,899 mice before her death in March 1987. Sales manager Peter Fairlie devotedly recorded the kills. A bronze statue was erected at the distillery in Towser's honour.

• • •

IN January 1985, a four-year-old dog from Dundee named Trixie reportedly blew up her owners' house by pulling off a pipe connected to the gas cooker, causing gas to pour into the kitchen. It was ignited by the pilot light and caused a huge explosion. Trixie and her owners escaped unharmed, but the house had to be rebuilt.

• • •

A grey squirrel set up home in St. Mary's Catholic Cathedral in Edinburgh in September 1998 and caused chaos. 'Cyril' the squirrel, as he was named, regularly made appearances during services. On 6 September alone, he was spotted drinking holy water from the font and dashing in front of the choir of St Andrew Camerata, as they performed. Several attempts to evict Cyril failed. Perhaps he is still in residence?

• • •

A pet sheep was found alive after being buried in a deep snowdrift for forty-five days. According to its owner, Dugald Wyper from Leochel Cushie, Aberdeenshire, the animal vanished after it was left outside during a storm on 22 January 1984. On 8 March, Wyper was out in the field where the sheep was entombed and thought he saw a rabbit's ears. It was only after a heavy fall of rain that day that he realised that it was no rabbit, but the ears of a sheep. Wyper believed that the sheep had survived because it was overweight and had lived on its fat. 'It is looking very thin and has lost about a third of its weight, but has started nibbling away at grass again.'

• • •

FOR some years, several large pythons and a boa lived peacefully in a cage in Edinburgh Zoo's Reptile House. But on the morning of 27 April 1934, the keeper found one less snake in the den: the boa was missing. It did not take him long to realise where the snake had gone. One of the pythons had attacked and swallowed the boa whole. It was a simple case of cannibalism and the culprit now lay enlarged by its meal. As an explanation for the attack on the snake's one-time companion, the keeper explained that the python had shed its skin during the night, as it did periodically, and being hungry and ready to feed, with no keeper nearby to tend to it, the reptile had made a meal of its nearest neighbour.

• • •

IT appears that a pigeon made a spectacular round trip to and from the Far East in July 1997. Jim Aitchison rescued an exhausted and soaked racing pigeon from a muddy puddle in the middle of a road in Pencaitland, East Lothian. The three-year-old female pigeon, belonging to a fancier in Denmark, had a note tucked inside her leg ring from a man living on an island off the coast of Java. Aitchison wrote to *The Indonesian* newspaper in the hope of confirming that the bird had travelled an astonishing round-the-world journey of 16,000 miles.

• • •

THE *Pall Mall Gazette* of 19 July 1923 published the story of a woman from near Inverness who, while returning home from the bank with £10 knotted in her handkerchief, saw a hare caught in a trap. She tried to strangle it with her handkerchief, but the hare managed to bound off with the money. The article concluded by saying that the entire population of Inverness was hunting the hare.

• • •

FUDGE the hamster made headlines in September 2006 when he found a new home in Scotland after making an incredible journey from Devon to Scotland via some of the country's premier golf courses. Fudge accidentally ended up in Scotland after flying from Devon hidden in his owner's golf bag. Once he was discovered, Kingsley Moyle put Fudge in a box and took him on a tour around some of the top

Scottish courses, including Gleneagles and Turnberry. On the last day of the holiday, Fudge again escaped and Moyle had to head home without him. When a new driver rented Moyle's hired car, the hamster was discovered in it. He became Fudge's new owner, with Moyle's blessing.

• • •

SAMUEL Bisset (1721–83) from Perth has a special place in the annals of show business. He was the first man to train a pig for the stage and his prize student was one from Belfast. The remarkable animal-trainer settled there in 1775 after a highly successful tour of Britain and Ireland with his menagerie of specially trained animal acts. Early in 1782 Bisset purchased a black piglet from Belfast market for three shillings. He spent nearly two years training the animal to do tricks.

In August 1783 'The Wonderful Pig' made its debut on stage in Ranelagh, Dublin. Its performance was nothing less than sensational. The pig apparently kneeled, bowed, spelled out names using cardboard letters, told the time, calculated numbers and pointed out the married and unmarried individuals in the audience. Bisset's 'Learned Pig', as it came to be known, was an instant hit with audiences and earned him a considerable amount of money. When Bisset moved his show to another part of the city, he forgot to seek the permission of the local magistrate, and a zealous policeman burst on stage and interrupted the show. He destroyed the showman's props and threatened to kill the pig and see that Bisset was jailed if they were ever seen in his district again.

The poor Scottish pig-trainer never recovered from the

shock of this ordeal and died in Newcastle-upon-Tyne a few weeks later, before he had had the chance to complete a tour of Britain with his amazing act. It was left to another man, a Mr Nicholson, to do that and to make his fortune. He bought Bisset's animals and carried on where his unfortunate predecessor had left off. The Learned Pig and its companion acts reached London in February 1785 and were an instant sensation, attracting huge crowds until the 'Wonderful Pig's' death in November 1788. This remarkable animal was such a celebrity that several newspapers carried its obituary.

• • •

A sheep due for slaughter at a meat factory in Ayr in January 1933 was found to have been fitted with a wooden leg. The animal was one of a consignment of animals for slaughter from the Dalmellington district. It had lost the greater part of its near foreleg and been fitted with a perfect replacement limb of rough-hewn wood by the sheep's ingenious owner. The sheep was in first-rate condition and had not suffered from its disability. The wooden leg was fourteen inches long. A deep carved socket fitted over the animal's stump and the base of the leg was a little more than two inches in diameter. Cloth that had been wound around the stump of the sheep's limb protected it and prevented friction occurring. The leg was held in position by a strap fastened around the sheep's body.

• • •

JOHN Ramsay from Perthshire found a deformed antler on a hill near Killiecrankie in June 1992 and sent a photograph of it to the *Fortean Times Magazine*. Ramsay said that the antler had recently been shed, adding that its loss must have been a huge relief to the animal. The freak antler was made up of the same material as an antler and weighed nearly eight pounds.

. . .

ANNA Buchan from Aberdeen was on her way to work in her mother's car in July 2008 when she felt something moving around in her trousers. The nineteen-year-old discovered a small bat inside them. 'I had no idea the bat was in there until I was sitting in the car. The movement must have woken him up because he began to move around,' she said. 'I was terrified and started screaming because I thought it was a wasp that was going to sting me. I couldn't believe it when I saw it was a bat. That's the last thing you expect to find in your trousers in the morning!'

It is thought that the tiny two-inch pipistrelle bat may have found its way into Anna's bedroom and used her wardrobe as a roosting place, taking up residence in her trousers. Overcoming her initial shock, Anna carefully took the creature in to work, where she placed it in a box. She rang the Scottish SPCA, who advised her that bats were a protected species and to release it back into the wild near her home that night.

• • •

DONALD Macarthur, a retired chief inspector, saw a lamb fall over a sixty-foot cliff in Dalbeg Bay on the Isle of Lewis in the Outer Hebrides in June 1990. When he investigated, he saw that the lamb had landed on a ledge halfway down the cliff and was unhurt, but he was unable to rescue it. Macarthur fetched the animal's owner, George Macleod. When they returned to the cliff, the lamb had gone and both men thought it had fallen into the sea. The next day, Macarthur observed the lamb on the summit of Stac na Gill, a rocky outpost seventy feet out to sea from the cliffs. Through binoculars, Macarthur saw that the lamb was happily grazing on the rock's grassy top. 'I couldn't believe it,' he said.

• • •

A parrot chewed through the power cable of his owner's computer and survived an electric shock strong enough to kill a human. James White from Loanhead, Midlothian, woke up on 11 February 2007 and did not know whether to laugh or cry when his fifty-year-old African Grey parrot, 'Mad Max', greeted him with a 'Hello'. After he had chewed through the cable, the electric shock had blown off all his feathers and left Max looking like a 'roast chicken'. When White tried to repair his computer the disgruntled parrot attacked him.

• • •

A letter in *The Times* on 25 September 1888 described how a toad had been found encased in a bed of clay on 15 September when workmen in Greenock were excavating a railway cutting. It was alive but inactive and so limp that it appeared to have no bones. Its legs could be bent any way. The letter said the frog had 'two beautiful eyes', but it did not appear to be able to see. Its mouth was sealed up, but it seemed to breathe very slightly through its nostrils, although how it breathed embedded in clay was a mystery. The writer calculated that the toad was between 20,000 and 30,000 years old.

• • •

On 25 May 2001, coastguards in Caithness were alerted to the sighting of an oil slick half a mile off Occumster. Two local fishermen investigated and found that the 'oil slick' was really a black mass of countless numbers of tiny drowned flies measuring about ninety-one by eighteen metres. The fishing boat was enveloped by a swarm of the tiny insects. An entomologist at the University of Aberdeen identified the species as St Mark's flies (*Bibia Marci*). They are long-legged hairy insects between twelve to fourteen millimetres long, which got their name because they usually appear on or near St Mark's Day (25 April). The flies on this occasion were far smaller than normal and a month late.

'None of us has ever heard of this sort of thing happening before,' said a university spokesperson. 'It's bizarre.'

• • •

THE National War Museum of Scotland at Edinburgh Castle has a curious exhibit on display: the varnished toenails of an elephant that the 78th Regiment had adopted as a mascot in the 1820s while it was serving in Ceylon (present day Sri Lanka). The elephant was brought back to Britain and resided at the castle until its death.

Unexpected Surprises

A codfish caught in the net of a Dundee fisherman in March 1874 was found to have swallowed a Bible. The leather-bound book was discovered in its stomach when the fish was being prepared for cooking. The book's title page was inscribed 'William Sim' with the date of 1830.

• • •

AN anxious passerby told Glasgow police at 1.30 am on the morning of 5 June 2000 that a live three-foot shark was thrashing about on the corner of Corunna Street and Argyle Street. By the time police arrived, the shark was dead.

• • •

CONNIE McCreath bought a packet of sliced bread at the Tesco store in Forres, Morayshire, in October 1997. Three days later it exploded on her kitchen work surface, sending a cloud of pink spores out of the hole that had been blown in the wrapper. The bread loaf was found to be too hot to touch. Mrs McCreath had bought the loaf on its sell-by-date.

• • •

WHEN his children asked Robert Henderson from Girvan in Ayrshire what he wanted for his golden wedding anniversary in 1952, his response startled them. 'A tombstone,' he replied. 'A nice big one, please, and put it up for me in the cemetery.' His dutiful children arranged for a headstone to be erected in the local cemetery. 'It's the best insurance policy I ever had,' Henderson said. 'I never felt better and I don't think I'll be needing it for a long time. But when I do, I know where it is.'

• • •

A hen belonging to Joe Green of St Andrews laid a strange egg for her master's breakfast in September 1950. It had a double yolk and between the two yolks was another egg complete with shell.

• • •

JOHN Napier from Fort William, Inverness-shire, was travelling by bus in April 1967 to visit his wife, who had just given birth to a son, when his Golden Labrador gave birth to five puppies on the bus during the journey. Napier acted as midwife to his dog.

• • •

THE Aberdeen fishing trawler *Eredene* made a strange catch in the North Sea on 5 April 1966: it landed a box of frozen filleted fish. The box must have fallen into the sea as it was being transferred from one boat to another.

• • •

BUTCHER Donnie MacKenzie from Newtonmore, Inverness-shire found the real life equivalent to the goose that laid the golden egg fairytale story. While preparing geese for sale in the run-up to Christmas in 1971, one of MacKenzie's employees noticed tiny sparkling objects like pinheads in the offal from one goose. An Edinburgh expert identified them as high quality gold particles that had been consumed by the goose while it was foraging in a stream. MacKenzie decided to keep the location of the stream a secret, to prevent any gold rush.

• • •

THERE was only one thing wrong with the three visiting Russian students who appeared on a television panel show on 5 December 1961 – they were Scottish! Three Aberdeen University medical students pulled off the amusing hoax with phoney names, broken 'Russian-sounding' English and plenty of nerve. They phoned the real students to say that the show had been cancelled because of a last-minute hitch, then showed up at the studio themselves pretending to be the Russians.

The hoax was discovered minutes after the show went on air, when some viewers rang in to say they had recognised the so-called 'Russians'. The real Russians were not amused and phoned their embassy in London to protest. They were told not to take the prank seriously.

• • •

PATRICIA McLeod from Bilston, Midlothian, was falling asleep one night in July 2003 when she started to hear an odd buzzing noise in one ear. Four hours later, the painful noise stopped. She went to see a doctor the next day, fearful that she was suffering from tinnitus, a condition that causes 'ringing' in the ears. The doctor thought her ear was blocked with wax and gave her almond oil to treat it. When Patricia returned four days later to have her ear syringed, a moth – nearly two inches long – was taken out of it.

· · ·

FISHERMEN in Campbelltown, Argyllshire made a catch of herring without even setting sail in January 1950. They spotted them under a steamer at the end of the quay, tossed their net over the side and landed the catch.

· · ·

AN attendant found a dead porpoise propped up in one of the cubicles of the men's toilets in Glasgow Central Station on 1 November 1965. The staff thought it was a dolphin, but the four-foot, sixty-four-pound carcass was identified as a porpoise by the museums department of Kelvingrove Park. How it got there nobody knew. One gentleman told *The Times*, 'We had heavy rain and there was flooding, but this is ridiculous.'

The porpoise was taken to Glasgow City Council's Museum, where the curator of the Department of Natural History said it was 'freshly caught' and that porpoises were quite common in the Firth of Clyde. He later arranged to have a fibreglass cast taken of the specimen.

• • •

IN 2007, Andy Lees from Blackburn, West Lothian, was diagnosed with terminal cancer. In September 2008, a year after their initial diagnosis, doctors at St John's Hospital in Livingston told Lees that he was in fact not suffering from cancer, but from chronic obstructive pulmonary disease. Although a serious condition, which had caused the airways to narrow, it was not fatal. Ironically, the news that he was not dying was a bitter blow to Lees since he had given away his life savings of £12,000 to family and friends. He also had spent another £6,500 on his funeral and was now penniless. Lee planned to sue his local health authority for the distress their misdiagnosis had caused.

• • •

A postcard mailed in 1889 finally reached its destination on 21 February 2001 – 112 years later. It was addressed to a Miss Wardrop of 32 Carden Place, Aberdeen, and had been posted on 4 January 1889, but had not left Australia until early 2001.

It read: 'Just a few lines to say I am still in Brisbane and have enjoyed my six weeks' leave. I reported myself today at the bank, but have not yet heard from my destination. Thanks awfully for letters from you and Gerty. Trusting you are all well and wishing you all a happy New Year. Will write in a day or two. This is the first time postcards have been issued in Queensland. Colin.'

The address at Carden Place was occupied by businesses and no one by the name of Wardrop lived in Aberdeen, so it initially looked as if no family members would be found. A few days later, seventy-four-year-old Alison Britts from New South Wales in Australia came forward to say the card had been sent by her grandfather, Colin Wardrop, to his sister Minnie. The 'Gerty' referred to their sister Gertrude. Wardrop later rose to become the head of the National Bank of Queensland. The card was later posted back to Ms Britts in Australia.

• • •

MANY strange things have been caught off the coast of Scotland as the following three examples illustrate.

Fishermen on the *Sharon Louise* were puzzled by the unusual weight of their net as they hauled in a catch 200 miles east of Peterhead in July 1987. Then a huge set of wheels and part of a lorry's undercarriage broke the water's surface. The fishermen were able to read the lorry's registration number before they cut the net.

The Aberdeen trawler the *Faithlie* was fishing off Scotland on 3 October 1963 when a unusually heavy catch was made. The net was so heavy the winch began to creak. The crew could not believe their eyes when a tusk broke the surface of the water, followed by another tusk, and then a trunk. They had caught an elephant sixty miles off Scotland! It was clear the elephant had been in the water for some time and they let it slide back into the sea. 'We were fishing near a regular trade route,' Captain Dale Simpson said. 'The only explanation is that the elephant had died in transit and had been dropped overboard. He is still floating out there somewhere.'

According to *The Sun* of 8 April 1982, another elephant was found in the North Sea thirty-two miles off Aberdeenshire when the crew of a trawler went to investigate what they thought was an overturned boat. Like the crew of the *Faithlie*, they too were surprised to find that it was a dead elephant.

• • •

THREE hitchhikers had no sooner thumbed a lift from a passing motorist near Alness in Ross in October 1971 than police stopped the car and arrested the Good Samaritan, hauling him away in handcuffs. He turned out to have escaped from a prison in the southeast of England.

• • •

WHEN the employees of a hairdressers on the top floor at 103a Princes Street in Edinburgh arrived for work on 17 April 1934, they saw signs that the premises had been burgled. The light was switched on and glass from a large fanlight lay broken on the floor. The police were called. It was quickly realised that nothing was missing and police on the roof discovered why – there had been no robbery. A ridge tile had been dislodged by the wind and masonry had fallen on to the fanlight, breaking it. A piece of broken glass had apparently hit the light switch, turning on the light.

• • •

THE world's oldest known bottle of Veuve Clicquot champagne, dating from 1893, was found hidden in a sideboard in Torosay Castle on the Isle of Mull in the Inner Hebrides by the castle's owner, Christopher James, in July 2008. For years James had wondered about what lay behind a locked secret panel in a sideboard at his family's ancestral home. When he took over the running of the castle, he hired a specialist locksmith to help him solve the mystery. Inside was a hidden drinks cabinet which contained the 1893 champagne, a bottle of brandy, a port decanter and a bottle of claret. Experts said the unopened 115-year-old bottle of champagne was 'literally priceless'.

The 'Torosay bottle', as it is now known, is believed to be the oldest surviving vintage of the famous champagne house and was in mint condition, having been safely locked away from sunlight. Unfortunately, the liquid inside is probably undrinkable because champagne does not usually last for longer than 30 years. James made a gift of the bottle to Veuve Clicquot and it is now on display in their visitor centre in Reims. 'I'm delighted the bottle is now on display in its rightful home,' James said. In return for his generosity, the company presented him with a case of its finest champagne.

• • •

YOU would think a woman would know when she is pregnant, but life is rarely so simple. Lorna Lowden of Aberdeen came home from work in November 1985 feeling unwell. Her husband Kenny, thinking it was appendicitis, called their doctor, who quickly diagnosed that she was pregnant and going into labour. With the doctor's help, Lorna gave birth to a boy, Craig, that same day.

• • •

SEVERAL strange objects have been found inside rocks. How they got there remains a mystery. Workmen quarrying stone near the River Tweed near Rutherford Mill in Raxton, Aberdeen-shire, in June 1844, discovered a piece of gold thread embedded in the rock eight feet below ground level. A small piece of the thread was sent to the offices of the local newspaper, the *Kelso Chronicle*, 'for the inspection of the curious'.

A nail partly embedded in a block of sandstone taken from the Kingoodie quarry near Dundee was described at a meeting of the British Association for the Advancement of Science in 1845. Sir David Brewster, who presented the report, said that about an inch of the nail was fixed firmly in the rock. The rest was projected into a layer of gravel, where it had rusted. Interestingly, it was the head of the nail that was embedded in the rock and the point that protruded. The depth from which the nine-inch-thick block of stone was removed was not stated, but the quarry was said to have been worked for twenty years before the discovery.

• • •

BUILDER Billy Hardy was knocking a hole in a wall at the Royal Museum of Scotland in Edinburgh in the summer of 1994 when he discovered fossils of a 336-million-year-old swamp tree hidden in the stone. When Hardy noticed the strange lines running through the sandstone, he informed the museum. Staff identified the marks as fossils of a lycopsid, a 'scale tree' that had grown in the carboniferous era. The trees grew up to thirty-five metres high and had trunks a metre across. Unusually, the lycopsids were supported by their tough bark, which was covered with needle-like leaves. The museum was built in 1889 with sandstone from Hermand Quarry in West Lothian. In carboniferous times, Scotland was near the equator and was covered in tropical swamps. Since Hardy's discovery, more fossils of the same species have been found in another wall of the Royal Museum.

• • •

IN November 2004, staff at Harvey Nichols in Edinburgh noticed that a large number of heavily pregnant women were loitering around the store with no apparent intention of buying anything. It emerged that there was an untrue rumour circulating in maternity classes and doctors' surgeries that the shop gave a £500 gift voucher to pregnant women who went into labour in the store. How this urban myth started remains a mystery.

• • •

ON 5 March 2003, a female shop assistant in the New Town area of Edinburgh was fooled into letting a man cover her feet with various tinned foods, including baked beans, and allowing him to take photographs of her feet. When the man claimed to be raising money for Comic Relief, she agreed to carry out the stunt. He asked her to close her eyes and guess what foods he was pouring over her feet. It was only when the woman told her friends what had happened that she realised she had been conned into doing something very silly. The man had claimed he was being sponsored, but there were no witnesses with him and he did not ask for money. Whatever his motives were, it was not a genuine attempt to raise money for the charity.

Fascinating Facts

THE first telegraph cable between Ireland and Britain was laid in 1853 between Donaghadee, County Down and Portpatrick, Dumfriesshire.

• • •

THE world's largest bottle of whisky was unveiled on 3 July 1987 when the six-foot-tall giant bottle was filled with 185 litres of Grant's Finest Scotch Whisky at the Glenfiddich Distillery at Dufftown, Banffshire.

• • •

PETER Grant from Braemar in Aberdeenshire was the last survivor of the 1745 Jacobite rebellion in Scotland. He died in 1824 at the age of 110. When George IV visited Edinburgh in 1822, he heard the story of Peter Grant, 'his oldest subject and oldest rebel', and granted him a pension of a guinea a week.

• • •

IN 1829, Glasgow merchant William Maclean advised the City Council to purchase the Plantation estate on the outskirts of Glasgow, which was then farmland. His advice went unheeded, so Maclean bought it himself for £15,000. Almost immediately, he sold a small portion of the land to a railway company for £30,000. Maclean received nearly as much again for another strip of land adjoining the River Clyde. The rest of the Plantation estate was sold bit by bit over the following decades, to the further enrichment of Maclean and his family.

• • •

A strong wind blew down a flagpole in Catrine, Ayrshire, in May 1970. The pole hit the town clock which had not worked for ten years and it started working again.

• • •

NEEDING money to fund a crusade in the Holy Land, King Richard the Lionheart effectively granted Scotland its independence in 1189 in exchange for a payment of 10,000 silver marks from King William I of Scotland.

• • •

DURING his time in Samoa in the 1890s, American diplomat Henry Clay Ide became friendly with the writer R.L. Stevenson. When Ide mentioned to Stevenson in passing how disappointed his young daughter Annie was that her birthday fell on Christmas Day, meaning that she had no separate birthday celebration, Stevenson drew up a formal deed of gift, properly sealed and witnessed as a legal document, donating his birthday (13 November) to Annie. She celebrated that date as her birthday until her death in 1945.

• • •

ON 13 October 1839, James Bryan from Ayrshire, who was apparently quite insane, presented himself at Windsor Castle as a suitor for the hand of Queen Victoria. He was abruptly dismissed.

• • •

THE world's oldest post office is in the town of Sanquhar in Dumfriesshire. The building on High Street has been operating continuously as a post office since 1712.

• • •

ELIZABETH Cockburn from Tillymauld near Turrif, Aberdeenshire, was aged 101 when she first got electricity installed in her cottage in August 2001. Remarkably, she had managed to live her entire life without the aid of an electrical appliance, Calor gas being her only source of power.

• • •

ALEXANDER Seton, 1st Earl of Dunfermline (1555–1622) was made Prior of Pluscarden Priory, near Elgin in Morayshire, at the age of ten in 1565. He held the office until 1577.

• • •

IN 1992, Stuart Thomson, who owned a small pet shop in the Shawlands district of Glasgow, ordered 120,000 plastic bags from a supplier in Xinjiang in western China. Once he had made the 120,000 bags, the manufacturer applied for an export grant from the Chinese government, taking advantage of a law giving businesses a subsidy for defective exports. The manufacturer simply changed the colour of the bags from white to yellow and printed a wrong phone number on the bags. Then he made millions of bags and raked in a large subsidy. The distinctive yellow bags, with a red parrot and the words 'The Pet Shop, 992 Pollokshaws Road, Glasgow' printed on them, spread across central Asia along the ancient Silk Road.

•   •   •

ALEXANDER Macarthur was one of seven brothers who fought at the battle of Culloden on 16 April 1746. He was the only one to survive it.

•   •   •

AMAZINGLY, bagpipes do not feature on the musical score of Mel Gibson's film *Braveheart*. Mel Gibson explains on his director's commentary on the *Braveheart* DVD why the haunting music features Irish uilleann pipes, rather than the more appropriate Scottish bagpipes: 'The uilleann pipes were just more melodic because the Scottish bagpipes tend to sound like a scalded cat. I just found the Irish pipes to be more romantic.'

Braveheart tells the story of William Wallace (c.1270-1305), a Scottish patriot, who led a campaign against the English occupation of Scotland. Uilleann pipes were invented at the beginning of the eighteenth century.

•   •   •

GLASGOW Bridgeton MP James Maxton set a record for frugality when he retained his seat in the general election of 1935 after spending only £54 on his re-election campaign.

• • •

THE world's tallest hedge is the Meikleour beech hedge in Perthshire, which was planted in 1746. Its height varies from eighty feet to 120 feet and is 1,804 feet long. The hedge is trimmed every ten years.

• • •

WHEN the Empire State building was still the tallest man-made structure in the world, an impromptu fight took place on 14 April 1932 on one of its top floors between a Scotsman and an Irishman who were working there, thus setting a record for the 'dizziest fight'. Charles Campbell and Patrick Dougherty worked as cleaners in the building and began to argue about who should first use a ladder balanced above the eighty-seventh floor. When the argument developed into a bitter spat and slurs were cast over the other's nationality, a fight ensued. Irishman Dougherty hit Campbell once, breaking the Scot's jaw. While Campbell was rushed to hospital, Dougherty was arrested for the assault.

• • •

FOR a bet, eight-year-old Jane Maxwell (1749–1812), later Duchess of Gordon, rode a sow through Edinburgh's High Street.

• • •

THE first bridge over the River Ettrick was built by famous Border Reiver Walter Scott (c. 1550-1629) of Harden, after a captive child kidnapped by his men drowned as they were crossing the ford when returning from a raid. Scott built a bridge of three arches in 1628 over the river near the village of Ettrickbridge End in Selkirkshire and set into the bridge a panel with his coat of arms carved on it.

• • •

IN about 1150, King David I of Scotland defined an inch as being the width of an average man's thumb at the base of the nail.

• • •

THE first balloon ascent in Britain or Ireland took place in Edinburgh on 27 August 1784. James Tytler (1745–1804) from Fearn in Angus briefly flew in a hot air balloon he had designed and built. It rose to a height of around 300 feet and drifted only about half a mile away before landing. Tytler's flight was so short because he could find no way to take a burner with him to keep the balloon airborne.

• • •

IN January 1957, an advertisement for a butcher's assistant in Glasgow advised applicants they 'must be able to cut, skewer and serve a customer'.

• • •

ADAM Smith (1723–90) from Kirkcaldy in Fife was a famous philosopher and economist. He is also notable for his last words, which were unintentionally macabre. He told his colleagues: 'I believe we must adjourn the meeting to some other place.'

• • •

WILLIAM Wilkinson Whitehead from Glasgow was known as 'The Giant Boy'. When exhibited at London's famous Bartholomew Fair in March 1825, he was aged fourteen and weighed a colossal twenty-two stone. Whitehead stood five feet, two inches high, and measured five feet around his body. The writer William Hone thought he was 'as fine a youth as I ever saw, handsomely formed, of fair complexion, and intelligent countenance, active in motion, and sensible in speech. He wore a plaid costume and a matching bonnet.'

• • •

IN 1836, five boys hunting for rabbits on Arthur's Seat found seventeen tiny coffins hidden inside a cave. Each coffin was four inches long and contained an expertly carved wooden figure inside with painted black boots and custom-made clothes. Nobody knows who made them or what they were meant to represent. One theory is that they commemorate the victims of the infamous murderers Burke and Hare. The coffins are as much a mystery now as when they were discovered and the eight that remain are on display in the Museum of Scotland in Edinburgh. The others have crumbled away.

• • •

WHEN Patricia Mugilston, a retired librarian from Aberdeen, died in 2004, she left a bequest of £10,000 to each of her two cats, Matilda and Top Cat.

• • •

THE Man of Feeling by Edinburgh writer Henry Mackenzie was published anonymously in 1771, and sold very well. Bizarrely, a young Irish clergyman named Charles Stewart Eccles tried to claim the novel as his own work, and even went as far as to back his claim with a manuscript in his own handwriting, complete with deletions, corrections and changes. MacKenzie and his publisher denounced this fraudulent claim and demonstrated the novel's provenance. When Eccles died, his tombstone repeated his false claims. Mackenzie was a prolific and versatile writer, but none of his works attained the success or controversy of *The Man of Feeling*.

•   •   •

IN August 1964, Sardinia's tourist office feted ninety-six-year-old John Cotterell from Glasgow as the island's oldest tourist that year.

•   •   •

MARGARET McDowall, born in Edinburgh in 1660, became a widow thirteen times. She buried all her husbands and lived to the age of 106.

•   •   •

ACCORDING to local lore, John Orr, the Laird of Bridgeton, near the village of St Cyrus in Aberdeenshire, saw a young couple struggling through snow drifts in the early 1800s and decided to do something about it. Thanks to a bequest in his 1844 will, four brides from the locality benefit from a dowry of £1,000 that Orr had established. The criteria for picking those to benefit from the fund is novel.

Each year the oldest, the youngest, the tallest and the shortest woman from the village who get married in St Cyrus receive a dowry from the money he left for that purpose. The annual interest is actually divided in five, with the fifth used for the benefit of the poor. Brides-to-be have their heights and ages recorded by the local minister before the wedding ceremony. The value of the dowry used to be equal to six months' wages for a rural worker, but the returns from the fund have diminished over time and now brides receive only an engraved vase as a gift.

Sporting Shocks

WHO needs a gun when you can just use a golf ball? While playing in the Edinburgh High Constables' Competition at Kilspindie in East Lothian on 10 June 1904, Captain Ferguson sent a long ball into the rough at the target hole. Ferguson found his ball and discovered that it had hit and killed a young hare. On 12 August 1975 (the first day of grouse shooting), eleven-year-old Willie Fraser of Kingussie, Inverness-shire, accidentally killed a grouse with his tee shot on the local course.

• • •

GORDON Brown from Troon had a tooth removed on 12 October 1970 without even opening his mouth. A surgeon removed it from his leg. Brown believed it had come from another player he had collided with several days before during a rugby match in Melrose, Roxburghshire. Twenty-two-year-old Brown said he had felt a pain in his left shin in the days following the game, but did not pay much attention to it until the wound started to fester. The tooth was discovered when an X-ray revealed an entire front tooth, root and all, buried in Brown's leg. Meanwhile, a player from the opposite team, Alistair Wilson, was said to be missing a tooth. Brown played for Scotland and was a member of the Lions.

• • •

BERT Campbell and Dave Young both scored holes-in-one at the same hole – the short ninth – in the same match at Ballochmyle Golf Club, Ayrshire in April 1985. After searching the area around the green, they found Campbell's ball in the hole, resting on top of Young's.

• • •

UNUSUALLY for a city of its size, Dundee supports two senior professional football teams, Dundee United and Dundee Football Club. Their grounds lie within a mere 160 metres of each other and are the closest professional football grounds in Britain.

Dundee man John Walsh was so fervent a supporter of Dundee Football Club that in June 1967, he named his new-born son John Arrol Hamilton Cox Murray Stewart Stuart Campbell Scott Wilson McLean Bryce Walsh after each of the eleven players on the club's team.

• • •

LOCAL man Gordon McFie made golfing history at Troon, Ayrshire, on 12 January 1933 at two of the town's golf courses. In a four-ball match on the Lochgreen course, he holed out in one at the third hole, a distance of 198 yards. Later in the day, playing in a three-ball game at the Darley course, he repeated the feat at the seventh hole, over a distance of 121 yards.

• • •

PATSY Gallacher enjoyed a successful career as a football player for Celtic. He famously scored one of the strangest goals ever recorded. During the 1925 Scottish Cup Final against Dundee, Gallacher ran into the box with the ball and wedged it between his heels. Then, with the Dundee defenders all around, Gallacher somersaulted over the goal line with the ball and into the net for a goal.

• • •

WHILE the British Open Golf Championship was held at St. Andrews in July 1957, a cat chased a mouse across the eighteenth green in the middle of the title play.

• • •

IN July 1954 an angler was fishing from an island on a river near Wigtown, in Wigtownshire, when he was caught in a rising flood. It was impossible to throw him a rope and the situation looked serious. Then along came golfer Robbie Murray, the Wigtown amateur champion, who had his golf clubs with him. He drove a nail through a ball, attached a piece of string to the nail and hit the ball across the water to the marooned angler. The string was tied to a strong rope, which was then hauled across by the angler, fastened to a tree and used to swing himself over to safety.

• • •

SOMETIMES golfers encounter unusual obstacles. In June 1907, Mr R. Andrew was playing for the Hillhouse Cup at

Troon and was forced to take ten strokes at a hole because his golf ball became impaled on a hatpin. Andrew was unaware he could have removed the hatpin without incurring a penalty.

On 25 September 1907, at the Royal and Ancient Golf Club in St. Andrews, Fife, a golf ball hit the hat of a lady crossing the fairway and stuck on the point of her hatpin.

• • •

RAITH Rovers beat Clyde at Kirkcaldy in the second round of the Scottish Cup on 11 February 1950, but never scored a goal. All three Raith goals were scored by members of the Clyde team who kicked the ball into their own goal.

• • •

SCOTSMAN Mike Rider was playing golf at a course in Palm Beach, Florida, on 12 November 1930, but failed to get a birdie, because of a birdie. Rider had just made a clean drive straight down the middle of about 225 yards when a buzzard swooped down, picked up the ball and flew away.

• • •

JIM Alder from Glasgow won the Commonwealth Games marathon in Kingston, Jamaica, on 11 August 1966, even though he lost his way and ended up running a greater distance than his competitors. The twenty-six-year-old hospital attendant nearly had victory snatched from him because of a blunder by the race organisers. Alder had a lead over his nearest rival, Englishman Bill Adocks, but there was no one waiting to direct him into the National Stadium when he reached it, and Alder took a wrong turn as he searched for the entrance.

While Alder was looking for a way in, Adcocks found the entrance and ran in to the stadium, surprised to be in the lead. He shrugged as if to say, 'It was nothing to do with me,' and began the final circuit of the track. Alder was finally directed into the stadium and discovered that he was now fifteen yards behind his rival. He refused to surrender the race and pushed hard past the tiring Englishman fifty yards from the line, going on to win the marathon in style by ten yards.

●   ●   ●

AFTER winning the 1970 US Open, English golfer Tony Jacklin returned to Britain, sent his trousers to be cleaned on 7 July and almost lost his $21,000 winner's cheque. Staff at a Dundee cleaning firm were getting the trousers ready for cleaning when the cheque fell out of a pocket. The manager sent it back to Jacklin, who was preparing to defend his British Open title.

The twenty-six-year-old golfer already thought the cheque had been banked. His wife Vivian accepted the blame. 'I usually look in the pockets of clothes sent to the cleaners,' she explained. 'I slipped up badly here!' Jacklin said that when he had been presented with the cheque at Chaska, Minnesota, two weeks before, he had put it in his pocket and forgot about it. 'It was hard work winning that cheque,' he said. 'I know where it is going now – straight into the bank.'

Criminal Cons

ORIGINAL thinking by a prisoner in Duke Street Prison, Glasgow, helped him escape on 20 January 1929. After eating his dinner, he told a warder that he had swallowed a spoon and pretended that he was in agony. The prisoner was immediately rushed to hospital, where, on examination, it was found that the story was a hoax. He was declared fit to go back to prison, but managed to escape on the return journey. A warder and the prisoner had headed back to the prison in a tramcar. The pair alighted from the car at Cathedral Square and were walking over to the prison gate when the man pushed the warder aside and dashed off. A large crowd had gathered in the square to watch the antics of students raising money for charity. The escaping prisoner mingled with them and got away.

• • •

JAMES Adams from Aberdeen became the first man in Scotland to be convicted by his toe prints in March 1953. Adams forgot the holes in his socks when he removed his shoes to break into a warehouse and the toe prints were enough to obtain his conviction and earn him a twelve-month spell in jail.

• • •

THE ocean liner *SS Cameronia* earned a speeding ticket on 11 June 1931 when the ship sailed down the river Clyde at a high rate of knots and created so great a wash that the surge of water broke the moorings of two ships tied up in the river basin. The ship's owners were fined a considerable sum.

• • •

AUTHORITIES at Barlinnie prison in Glasgow banned inmates playing soccer in December 1952. Since May of that year, eleven prisoners (a whole team in a sense!) had escaped while matches were being played on the soccer field outside the prison walls.

• • •

TORVALD Alexander arrived home in Inverleith, Edinburgh, from a New Year's fancy dress party on 1 January 2009 dressed as Thor, scaring the living daylights out of an opportunistic burglar. Alexander was dressed as the Norse God of Thunder, with a red cape, silver-winged helmet and a breastplate. When he spotted the burglar in his front room, rifling through a desk, Alexander charged at him.

The man threw himself out of a first-floor window and escaped. 'As soon as he saw me, his eyes went wide in terror,' Alexander said. 'He looked like he'd had a few drinks and decided to do a late-night break-in, but he hadn't counted on the God of Thunder living here.'

The burglar had not managed to steal anything and left his shoes behind when he fled. Alexander handed them over to the police in the hope that they would help them find the burglar.

• • •

ON 1 December 1952 an expert safecracker broke out of Saughton jail in Edinburgh using only a pen. Hugh Kelly Mannion, who had broken into the same jail in 1949 to rescue a friend, made good his escape by rewriting bail papers and calmly walking out of the gates. It took fifty hours before the forgery was discovered. Officials said that Mannion, who was awaiting trial on safe-stealing charges, had got hold of another prisoner's bail bond in the sheriff's office and had put his own name on it.

• • •

PERTH police finally solved the two-year-old mystery of a series of thefts of kilts in August 1971. For two years a thief had been stealing kilts from Boy Scout huts, backstage dressing rooms and dry-cleaning delivery trucks. When they tracked George Shields, a thirty-one-year-old dishwasher, to a derelict house, they searched the building and found a large number of kilts. A prosecuting solicitor told the court that Shiels was fascinated by Highland dress, but could not afford to buy kilts. He was remanded in custody while a background report was prepared. He wore trousers in court and pleaded guilty.

• • •

GREENOCK policemen spotted a man stealing from a doctor's car in January 1969 and gave chase. The thief jumped over a wall and thumbed a lift from an approaching car. As the driver opened the door for him, he noticed – too late – that it was a police car. The unlucky thief was jailed for six months.

• • •

AFTER crashing into another car in November 1973, Glasgow man Tom Barnett fled and sped to his nearby home, quickly shaved off his distinctive moustache and returned to the scene, saying his car had been stolen. Barnett's lie was seen through when an observant policeman taking witness statements about the runaway driver spotted a fleck of shaving soap under Barnett's nose and arrested him. The forty-eight-year-old was later convicted of drunk driving.

• • •

IN November 2003, jewel thief Giuseppe Cannata asked to see a diamond worth £20,000 in Clelland Brown Jewellers on Rose Street, Edinburgh, and managed to switch it for a worthless fake. He had made his getaway before staff realised what he had done. Cannata was caught when he had the bad luck to board a train for London and was spotted by the jewellery store owner, who was sitting in the same compartment. He alerted police and the thief was arrested when the train arrived in London. Cannata had the diamond hidden on his person.

• • •

CRIMINALS were no less ingenious in past times than their present-day counterparts. Just before Sutherland's confectionery shop on Inverkin Street in Greenock, Renfrewshire, closed on 26 February 1933, two men arrived with a heavy tea chest for Wood's tobacconist shop next door, which had already closed. They asked if they could leave the box there so Wood's would have the box first thing the next morning. The shop girl allowed them to leave the box in the shop and then closed up for the day. When the girl arrived the next morning, she was amazed to see that the box, which had been tightly tied with rope, was empty. Alarmingly, the back door was open and the till had been rifled. Police believed that a boy had hidden inside the box and had cut his way out as soon as the shop was shut.

• • •

SIR Robert Strange (1721–92) led a charmed existence. His life was once saved by a woman's skirts. The noted artist was a fervent Jacobite and supporter of Bonnie Prince Charlie. Following the failure of the 1745 Rebellion, Strange was outlawed by the authorities and went on the run. He was in hiding for several months and eked out a living by drawing portraits of Prince Charlie and leading Jacobites. While he was staying at his fiancée Isabella Lumisden's house in Edinburgh, soldiers came looking for him. Isabella acted quickly to save him. She lifted her hooped skirt and hid her outlawed fiancée beneath it. Then she sat in a chair – with Strange curled up in hiding beneath her. When the soldiers entered, she calmly continued her needlework and sang Jacobite songs while they searched the house. Isabella and Robert married in 1747. He was knighted by King George III in 1787.

• • •

HOURS after he had stolen it, a thief tried to use a credit card in an Edinburgh supermarket and was unlucky enough to be served by his victim's mother. The thief stole the card after breaking into a parked car in Silverknowes in March 1999. He then tried to use it for his shopping at a Safeway store in the city. The cashier serving him immediately recognised that it was her son's missing credit card and secretly raised the alarm.

• • •

ON 15 March 1997, 1,000 cat's eyes were stolen from the busy A75 Gretna to Stranraer motorway in a brazen raid. The thieves dressed up as road workers and lifted the eyes from an area where safety work was in progress. Genuine workmen discovered the theft. A Dumfries police official said: 'It is the first time we have been faced with a crime like this.

And we don't really know what they will do with all these cats' eyes.'

• • •

AN armless man was found guilty of murder in an Edinburgh court on 27 October 1919. Despite having no arms, fifty-five-year-old William Lamb made a livelihood playing an organ on the streets of the city, working the instrument with his feet. Lamb was condemned to death for killing a woman with whom he lived, but was subsequently reprieved and given a life sentence instead.

• • •

WILLIAM Agnew from Stirling must surely have been one of the last persons charged with a unique traffic violation. The fruit merchant was fined £3 on 8 September 1969 for being drunk while in charge of a horse. The prosecutor, James Cochran, said it was the first such case for thirty years in Stirling and added that it used to be said 'that the horse always got them home'.

• • •

IN January 1953, it was reported that wily Glasgow entrepreneurs were making a profit by selling money! They were cashing in on a shortage of shilling pieces (worth 5 pence) by selling them for 15 pence. Housewives needed the coins to put into gas meters.

• • •

A judge excused an English woman from jury duty in March 1968 in a Glasgow murder case when she confessed that she was unable to follow the evidence. 'I can understand my own people, but I cannot understand some Scottish voices,' she said.

• • •

AN Edinburgh robber, who told a taxi driver to wait while he held up an off-licence, was jailed for sixteen months in August 2008. Steven Craig hailed a taxi around nine o'clock at night on 13 May and asked the driver to stop at the Victoria Wine store on Easter Road. Then he ran into the shop with a scarf over his face while the driver looked on. After threatening staff and stealing £200, he left the shop and boarded a bus while the taxi sat waiting.

• • •

JAMES McGlashan Walker of Newburgh, Fife, stole a car from a parking place in Perth on 10 August 1935, then drove over five miles to Auchtermuchty and tried to park it in a garage, out of sight. Unfortunately, he picked the same garage where the car's owner, Auchermuchty native James McKendrick, normally kept his car! After his car had been stolen, McKendrick reported its loss to the police, who circulated a description of the vehicle throughout Fife and Perthsire. He also phoned the garage in Auchtermuchty to let them know.

As he was speaking to the clerk at the garage, she said, 'I hear your car outside,' and ran downstairs to investigate. Sure enough it was McKendrick's car being driven into the garage by the unlucky thief. She confronted the man, who abandoned the car and ran off. A few days later Walker was arrested, tried and jailed for the theft.

• • •

EDINBURGH bachelor Patrick Ward was jailed for nine months in September 1960 for defrauding the tax office of £653 by claiming allowances for a fictitious wife and four children. The prosecutor pointed out that Ward claimed he had married in 1941, but he was born in 1930.

• • •

GLASGOW police appealed to the press on 15 July 1957 to challenge a boy's story that he had been tied up and burned by a gang, because his lie was giving the city a bad name. They said Sammy Trimble's story that youths had seized him a few nights earlier, poured turpentine on him, then roped him to an oil drum and set him alight, was untrue. The truth came out that the nine-year-old and his brother Billy had set fire to papers in an oil drum. When flames shot out, Sammy was seriously burned on his hands, chest and face.

• • •

AN Edinburgh youth who worked for a milk company found himself in the juvenile court on 7 December 1960 and admitted that he had stolen and drunk twenty-one pints of milk. The boy stressed that the milk came from a rival company.

• • •

A curious mystery became public knowledge in April 1997. For the previous eighteen months, a man posing as a street lighting officer in Tranent, East Lothian, had been turning on the town's streetlights during the day. The mysterious man broke into control boxes at night and jammed the control timers which automatically turned the lights off in the morning. He then resealed the boxes, leaving the lights on all day and causing an expensive headache for East Lothian Council. All attempts to trap the man failed and his motive remains a mystery. What is not in doubt is that the man dressed in a regulation fluorescent jacket, had a set of keys allowing access to the lighting controls and had inside knowledge. Scottish Power drew a blank when it investigated all its current and former employees. By April 1997, the man's actions had cost the council £7,000.

• • •

A Perth man's thrifty ways landed him in trouble in September 1952. Police caught Alexander McPhee carrying off scrap iron that he could not bear to see wasted. Unfortunately, it belonged to someone else. McPhee was let off with a light fine of £1, which he paid out of two handfuls of change he carried in his pockets, slowly counting out the sum in pennies.

• • •

DUNDEE police were puzzled by reports of driverless cars motoring through the city on 15 October 1970. When a police patrol encountered one of these cars, the mystery was solved. Inside the car was a driver – all three feet of six-year-old Stephen Peters. The boy had disappeared from school at lunchtime and was not seen until police caught up with him nine hours later. In that time, Peters had 'borrowed' three cars and driven them around the city. The six-year-old's first trip began when he reversed a car from a garage and drove it for two miles through busy intersections and on to the main route around Scotland's fourth biggest city.

•   •   •

THE last time a person was whipped through the streets of Glasgow was on 8 May 1822 when Richard Campbell was punished, receiving twenty lashes each at the jail, the Stockwell-foot, the Stockwell-head and Glasgow Cross by the hangman. He was also sentenced to transportation to Australia. His crime was to have been the ringleader of a riot.

•   •   •

MRS Alice Coyle appeared in an Edinburgh Court on a charge of drunkenness for the 235th time in December 1960. The judge let her off with a warning.

•   •   •

ON 11 February 1925 a thirteen-year-old Glasgow schoolboy was found lying in an ashpit near his home on Jamieson Street in the city's Govanhill district. The boy was discovered by a woman who had gone to empty her ash-pan. It had been raining and she was surprised to see the boy lying drenched and thought he was a poor homeless boy sleeping rough. Then she saw that his nostrils were plugged and his hands and feet tied together. A piece of string was wrapped around the boy's neck. The woman quickly informed the authorities and the bruised and exhausted boy was brought to the Victoria Infirmary.

John Miller told police that he had been attacked by two men who had robbed him of four shillings. Then they had gagged and tied him and flung him into the ashpit. The police were not satisfied with Miller's strange story and questioned him again. Finally the boy admitted that the whole thing was a hoax. He had read a detective novel called *The Australian Wild* and decided he would create a sensation about himself.

Odd Eccentricities

THOMAS Clark (1751–1817) from Dundee was so prudent that he lived on oatmeal stirred in hot water, which he begged from neighbours to save the cost of boiling it himself. Clark was once prescribed a dose of castor oil as a remedy for an illness, but he decided to swallow a lump of soap, reasoning that it did the same thing as castor oil and was far cheaper.

• • •

IN 1807, a wealthy Scotsman left an eccentric and original will. In it, he left each of his two daughters their weight in £1 bank notes. The women were duly weighed and then received their inheritance. The elder daughter weighed seven stone, two pounds and the younger eight stone. As a result, the heavier daughter received £57,344, while her older sister got £51,200. It was calculated that 512 £1 bank notes weighed a pound and the sisters' inheritance was reckoned on that basis.

• • •

SUSANNA Countess of Eglinton (1690–1780) was a famous society hostess in her day. When over eighty, she was still known for her beauty and told people she had never used make-up, but washed her face regularly with sow's milk. The countess lived her final years at Auchans, near Dundonald in Ayrshire, and was noted for the eccentric hobby of keeping tamed pet rats that came for food when she tapped on an oak wall panel of her dining room and opened a small door. We are told that ten or twelve rats would come out and eat. Then, at a word of command from the countess, they would retire.

• • •

BETWEEN 1792 and 1806, the schoolmaster of New Abbey near Dumfries was the miserly Robert Farries, who wore only clothes he had taken off scarecrows.

• • •

EDINBURGH judge Francis Garden, Lord Gardenstone (1721–93), was so fond of a pet pig that he let it sleep on his bed when it was a piglet. When the animal grew too large to share the bed, Garden allowed it to sleep in his bedroom on clothes he had taken off before going to bed and made into a comfortable pile for the pig. The peer was heard to remark how pleasant it was to have his clothes nice and warm in the morning when he put them back on.

During the 1745 Jacobite Rebellion, Garden and a companion got drunk in a Musselburgh pub, instead of doing their duty, and were captured by an enemy patrol. They were reputedly about to be hanged, but were released when it was clear they were drunk and more of a nuisance to their own side than to the enemy.

• • •

ARCHIBALD Campbell Fraser of Lovat (1736–1815) became eccentric towards the end of his life. He was visiting his friends the Macphersons one day when he started to build a nest of straw in his carriage outside his host's home at Cluny. He placed turkey eggs in it and sat on them in an effort to hatch them. Fraser left the nest only once or twice a day and during one of these absences the eggs were replaced with young chickens, which satisfied the old man.

• • •

JOCK Aird (1805–91) was a travelling beggar and musician for hire from Kirkmichael, Perthshire. His 'uniform' was an old dress hat and a cast-off policeman's coat. Inside the silk hat, Aird stored away chunks of bread and cheese for his travels.

• • •

AFTER her death in 1945, thirty-one incomplete or unsigned wills were found at the home of Miss Annie Moon in Fife. This legal mess meant that it would take another four years before the matter of her estate could be cleared up. Finally in April 1949, the Edinburgh Court of Sessions found that Miss Moon had last made a valid will in 1941 and her £51,000 estate could be divided according to its contents. Miss Moon was described in court as a 'lady with a hobby of making wills'.

• • •

IN the early nineteenth century, Montrose in Angus had only one letter carrier who was not 'noted for speed of foot'. David Pole was remarkable because he had a limp and always walked on his tiptoes, to save the soles of his boots.

• • •

WILLIAM Wilkie (1721–72), from Echlin, Linlithgow, was a poet known as 'The Scottish Homer' after he published an epic poem called the *Epigoniad*, styled after Homer's *Iliad*. Wilkie was also an eccentric. He liked to sleep with twenty-four blankets heaped on his bed and once astonished his hosts by insisting that they supply him with a pair of dirty sheets. Although an educated man, he could not spell or read well. Fortunately, that did not stop him from being appointed Professor of Natural Philosophy at the University of St Andrews in 1759.

He also found the time to take holy orders but was notoriously absent-minded. The reverend frequently forgot to remove his hat while preaching and was known to slip out of the church before the service was over. It is said that on one occasion he forgot to consecrate the bread and wine before distributing Holy Communion.

• • •

JAMES Wattie (1789–1872) was parish schoolmaster of Crimond in Aberdeenshire from 1813 to 1856 and was an eccentric dresser. He always wore several layers of flannels and greatcoats, along with a heavy cloak, even at the height of summer.

• • •

EDINBURGH-born Robert Hamilton (1743–1829) was an absent-minded professor of mathematics at Aberdeen University. Each morning a servant would check to ensure that Hamilton was fully dressed before he set off to teach. Hamilton loved mathematics. When he was appointed to the chair of natural philosophy at Aberdeen in 1799, he discovered that the university's professor of mathematics, a Mr Copland, preferred philosophy, so in a private deal they switched jobs. Hamilton unofficially held the position for seventeen years until he was finally appointed to the chair of mathematics in 1816.

• • •

ONE odd eccentric was Andrew Whitton, who died in Overgate, Dundee, in May 1903. He took a room as lodgings in the city in 1884 and never set foot outside the house from that time or allowed a fire to be lit in his room at any time of the year. Whitton never spoke to any other people in the house, but spent his time copying the names of people into dozens of books. He also owned a photographic album containing the pictures of ladies, 'whose features he would frequently study'. Despite his oddities, he was a good tenant and paid his rent regularly. He left an estate of £800, which went to the Crown.

• • •

DR George Fordyce (1736–1802) from Edinburgh was a famous figure of his time in London where he was highly regarded as a physician, even if he was a little eccentric. On one occasion the doctor was called to the sick bed of a wealthy lady who had suddenly taken ill. Dr Fordyce had had too much to drink and was unable to locate his patient's pulse. He cursed himself, muttering, 'Drunk, by Jove,' and wrote the patient a prescription for a harmless medicine. The next day he received a note from the patient confessing that his diagnosis had been correct and she rewarded the doctor with £100 for his silence.

Dr Fordyce was also renowned for following the same routine for twenty years without fail. At four o'clock every afternoon he went to Dolly's Chophouse in Paternoster Row and ate one-and-a-half pounds of rump steak along with half a chicken or a plate of fish. This was washed down by a tankard of strong ale, a bottle of port and a quart of brandy. Fordyce's routine was not cheap because the establishment was an expensive one where patrons were happy to pay inflated prices to eye the beautiful female staff. After leaving Dolly's, Dr Fordyce went to three coffee houses, one after another, taking a brandy and water at each before returning home. It is little wonder he died of gout at the age of sixty-six.

• • •

'PETTICOAT Dan' Cooper (1835–1913) is probably Kirkintilloch's best-known native. He was famous for not wearing trousers and for dressing in a rough petticoat, which earned him his nickname. Cooper was a much-loved and respected character who earned a living doing odd jobs around the town. He was a simple soul, but an important feature of Kirkintilloch. His obituary in the *Kirkintilloch Herald* in February 1913 blamed an attack of 'Rheumatic fever when he was two years old that left him mentally and physically infirm'. It also says Petticoat Dan's distinctive dress was necessitated by a physical infirmity. He wore 'a man's tweed jacket, a woman's skirt of coarse blue material, reaching down to his heels, and a rough packsheet apron'. Cooper featured in many picture postcards of the era.

Miracles of Life

A British Navy pilot, whose parachute failed to open properly, ejected himself from his Scimitar jet aircraft on 23 November 1962, fell 550 feet and escaped unhurt. Fortunately for twenty-three-year-old Lieutenant Christopher Legg, his seat had its own small parachute, which opened, stayed with him almost to the ground and helped to cushion his fall. 'I hardly felt anything,' he said. Legg landed in a stubble field near Elgin, Morayshire, and was pronounced practically unhurt after a medical check-up. The plane was not so lucky – its wreckage was scattered over a quarter of a mile.

• • •

IN the eighteenth century Margaret Dixon from Musselburgh, Lothian was found guilty of murdering her infant child and was sentenced to be hanged. Her execution took place in Edinburgh in November 1728. After her body had been hanging on the gallows for the prescribed length of time, it was cut down, put in a coffin and sent back to Musselburgh to be buried.

Two miles from Edinburgh the persons who were transporting the coffin on a horse and cart stopped for refreshment at a village called Peffermill. One of them saw the coffin lid move. When he lifted the lid, Margaret Dixon sat up and most of the amazed onlookers fled in terror. Wiser heads carried her into the pub, put her to bed and sent for a doctor. The next morning she was well enough to walk home. Under Scottish law, the sentence of death had been carried out and Margaret Dixon was legally dead, so the authorities did not return her to the scaffold. Her death also freed her from the bonds of marriage. A few days later, she publicly remarried her husband and was still alive in 1753 and pleading her innocence. In all probability her only crime was to have suffered a miscarriage.

• • •

WILLIAM Kellock (1632–1743) was town clerk of Sanquhar in Dumfriesshire for ninety-six years. He had all his faculties until the day he died, aged 111. He never wore glasses.

• • •

STEEPLEJACK George Armstrong had a lucky escape while repairing 468-feet-high Townsend's Stalk in Glasgow in September 1922. While working at a height of ninety feet, he tumbled and fell. At the base of the stalk was a tank ten feet deep, full of water. It was open at the top except for iron bars three feet apart. Incredibly, Armstrong missed the bars and landed in the water tank, escaping with only minor injuries. For many years, Townsend's Stalk was the tallest chimney in the world. It was demolished in 1927.

• • •

IRONICALLY, the tragic fate of eight airmen saved two climbers. When descending from the peak of Beinn Eighe in Wester Ross in December 2008, experienced climbers Ian Parnell and Jon Winter were hit by an avalanche and swept down a gully towards a cliff edge and a 1,200 foot drop.

The men were roped together and they were saved from almost certain death when Parnell hit the propeller of a Lancaster bomber that had crashed into the mountainside just fifteen feet below the summit on 13 March 1951, killing all on board. (It took six months for Royal Marines to recover the bodies of all eight crew members and the almost inaccessible crash site, west of Triple Buttress, was named Fuselage Gully.) Nearly sixty years later the two men were saved when Parnell hit one of the eight foot-long propeller blades and clung to it.

• • •

A three-year-old boy who hurtled over a sixty-foot cliff in a runaway wheelbarrow in May 1934 survived with hardly any injuries. Thomas Watson from Dysart, Fife, was playing with his two brothers and several friends on the grassy plateau known as the Engine Brae, which overlooks the Firth of Forth. He was sitting in a two-wheeled barrow, which was being pushed by his six-year-old brother, when a wheel caught in a rut and the barrow wheeled over on to a slight slope leading to the cliff's edge. The handles were torn from his brother's hands and the wheelbarrow raced down the hill and went over the edge, crashing on to the rocks below. Some men walking nearby rushed to where the child lay prostrate, but were astonished to find that he was only bruised.

• • •

ELIZABETH Gray died in Edinburgh on 2 April 1856, aged 108 years – 128 years after the death of her oldest brother. She was the daughter of the writer William Gray of Newholm and her birth is recorded in the parish records of Dolphington in Lanarkshire as having taken place in May 1748. Longevity was common to the females in her family. Her mother lived to be ninety-six and two of her sisters lived to the ages of ninety-four and ninety-six respectively. Her half-brother died as a child in 1728.

• • •

DURING a fox hunt in the parish of West Kilbride, Ayrshire on 8 January 1811 a young man fell from a place called the Three Sisters, the highest point of the Arneil Bank ridge. He dropped a distance of 130 feet and landed on a bed of small stones. Rescuers were amazed to find him alive with no bones broken, but badly bruised and in shock. Three days later he was well enough to be able to walk five miles.

• • •

CASTLE Fraser in Sauchen, Aberdeenshire, has several objects of interest belonging to Colonel Charles Mackenzie Fraser (1792–1871) on display. During the Napoleonic Wars, Mackenzie Fraser was a Captain in the Coldstream Guards at the siege of Burgos in Spain on 23 September 1812, where he received a wound to the head from a musket shot during the storming of the castle of Burgos. His life was saved by the cockade, a folded silk handkerchief in his hat. He narrowly escaped death when the musket shot pushed its way through the velvet cover, the hat and the lining and stopped close to his head. This lucky hat is on display in the dining room of Castle Fraser.

Later on in the battle, Mackenzie Fraser's luck ran out and he was shot in the knee by another musket ball, which could not be removed. Despite the best efforts of the doctor of the 3rd Regiment of Guards, which included treatment by bleeding and leeches, his leg had to be amputated some weeks later. Mackenzie Fraser returned home to his lands fitted with a wooden leg, but never allowed it to interfere with his life. He married, became an MP for Ross and Cromarty, and was made a Colonel of the Ross-shire militia. The two lead balls that struck MacKenzie Fraser are on display in the library, as is his wooden leg.

• • •

COLONEL James Gardiner (1687–1745) from Carriden, Linlithgowshire, was wounded fighting at the battle of Ramillies in present-day Belgium on 23 May 1706, during the War of the Spanish Succession. The nineteen-year-old officer was leading his men into action and was shouting encouragement to them when he was hit. A bullet passed through his open mouth, without touching or wounding his teeth, tongue or palate and went out through his neck about an inch and a half to the left of his vertebrae. Gardiner survived his wounds and went on to have a distinguished career in the army. He lived for another thirty-eight years and died at the battle of Prestonpans, Lothian, on 21 September 1745.

• • •

ACCORDING to the *Gentleman's Magazine* of September 1749, a 'poor chairman's wife, aged about seventy, was lately delivered of a child, which thrives, and is suckled by the mother, who never had one before; her husband is about her age.'

• • •

MESSAGES in bottles are traditionally sent in moments of extreme distress by sailors, but one saved the life of a desperate man on dry land in August 2003. Robert Sinclair had lived rough in the Stirlingshire countryside for the previous twenty-seven years, but after suffering from an asthma attack in a remote deserted farmhouse in Lethalian, near Falkirk, he was too ill to seek help. The fifty-seven-year-old lay there for seven days with nothing to eat or drink. Sinclair scribbled a note on a piece of cardboard, put it in an old plastic water bottle and dropped it out of the window of the house. The bottle was found by Ben, a border collie from a farm three miles away, and he took it to his master, Brian Besler.

'Ben found this bottle and came running up to me with it in his mouth,' Besler recalled. 'There was a message in it asking for help. I thought it was a wind-up until I saw the name – Robert's well known round here. It said he was ill, he couldn't breathe right, his chest was clogged up and he'd run out of food and water.'

Sinclair made a full recovery in Falkirk Royal Infirmary.

• • •

A well-made pair of jeans saved the life of twenty-year-old Derek Boyce in April 1992. He got stuck between floors in a broken lift in an Edinburgh tower-block. Rather than wait to be rescued, he decided to climb out through the lift's emergency hatch. Another lift that was passing by knocked Boyce off balance and he fell down the shaft. Ten storeys above the ground, his jeans snagged on a protruding stanchion and he was caught like a coat on a hanger. Although residents heard his calls for help, Boyce had to hang head down for another hour before rescuers were able to free him. He was taken to hospital with head and leg injuries.

• • •

JOHN Stewart of Dillievard, Angus, died on 29 May 1754 at the age of 105. He married his second wife at the age of eighty. She bore him ten children, the last of whom was born in his hundredth year.

• • •

ANDREW Duffy from Mansfield, East Calder, survived being run over by a three-ton road roller on 30 March 1998. The accident occurred while Duffy was laying a car park at Harmeny School in Balerno. The roller, he said, seemed to come out of nowhere. It knocked him down, face first, into the tarmacadam and kept rolling. As he lay sprawled, the unfortunate man could not escape the nightmarish turn of events.

Duffy remained fully conscious as the machine's two rollers slowly ploughed over him. He was rushed to the Edinburgh Royal Infirmary and placed on a ventilator in the intensive care unit. His life was saved solely because he had been pressed down into the soft tar. If it had been a hard surface, Andrew Duffy would have died. His main injuries were a broken leg, broken ribs and, most seriously, a fractured skull. In the circumstances, he got off lightly. Ten days later he was released from hospital and into the care of his family.

The brave man's recovery was slow and painful. For a long period he suffered from pain, dizziness and deafness and found it hard to walk, but he fought on and was back at work several months later.

• • •

CONSTRUCTION worker Tom Marie fell from the fourteenth floor of a building he was working on in Dundee on 4 March 1967 and survived. The forty-three-year-old dropped more than 150 feet, but managed to walk away with only minor injuries to his ear, wrists and hands. Marie fell when scaffolding gave way, but he was lucky enough to land on a pile of soft earth.

• • •

WHEN his parachute failed to open properly, Craig Paton from Kilmarnock fell 3,200 feet but miraculously survived the fall, suffering from chest injuries and internal bleeding, but no broken bones. It was the twenty-six-year-old's first parachute jump; he was a last-minute substitute on a jump some friends were doing for charity on 7 April 2001 at Strathallan Airfield near Auchterarder, Perthshire.

Paton's main chute opened only partially and his back-up became entangled in the main chute. As he came down, Paton bounced off a tree and on to a soft wet grassy embankment, just missing a fence and a road. When they reached him, police were astonished that he was still alive and able to ask them what had happened. Paton left hospital after just two weeks.

A few days after Paton's accident, another young Scot survived a similar fall when his parachutes failed to deploy properly and also became entangled. Twenty-six-year-old paratrooper Stuart Pearson, from East Kilbride, Lanarkshire, was on holiday with friends in the Israeli resort of Eilat and survived a 1,000 foot fall. Pearson landed on relatively soft sand dunes which cushioned his fall and he suffered only a broken thigh bone.

• • •

EWAN MacDonald, a young recruit in a Highlanders regiment, was executed for murder – twice! The nineteen-year-old was hanged in Newcastle on 28 September 1752. After the body had been cut down and moved to the nearby Surgeons' Hall for dissection, the surgeons were called away to attend a patient at the infirmary. When they returned, they discovered that MacDonald had revived and was strong enough to sit up. He begged for mercy, but a young surgeon, anxious not to be deprived of the opportunity of dissecting, killed MacDonald with a mallet.

• • •

ON 22 September 1950, James Riddoch from Keith in Banffshire fell into a binder, came out in a bale of oats and survived. The boy was riding on the machine when he slipped and fell onto the conveyor belt. He went into the binder and emerged bound with twine in a bale of oats. James was rushed to hospital suffering from a chest injury and extensive bruises.

• • •

STUART Taylor from Orkney was standing on the balcony of his apartment in Port Harcourt, Nigeria, in July 2007, sending a text on his mobile phone, when he was hit by gunfire. His phone stopped the bullet and saved his life. 'I didn't realise what it was until I felt a pain in my chest and I had trouble breathing,' he said. It took him a second or two to realise what had happened. 'I went back inside and got the driver to take me to the clinic. On the way, I phoned my manager and said I thought I had been shot.' After passing through the phone, the bullet hit Taylor's chest before exiting under his arm. If the phone had not slowed the bullet, Taylor could have been killed.

• • •

IDENTICAL twins Isabella and Marion Weir threw caution to the wind and had a drink to celebrate their 100th birthday on 29 September 1986, when they celebrated the occasion at a party attended by family and friends. Guests brought them flowers, gifts and a birthday cake with ten candles. The other ninety were on a table decoration. Isabella and Marion were fittingly dressed for their birthday in identical blue dresses they had knitted themselves. They lived together in their cottage on Main Street in the village of Longridge, East Lothian, and had never married.

The only time they were apart was when Marion went to Australia in 1911 at the age of twenty-five to work as a waitress in the dining room of a bank. Isabella joined her eleven years later, but they returned to Longridge in 1950. The *Guinness Book of Records* said the odds against identical twins reaching the age of 100 was 700 million to one. Marion died in March 1988 and less than a year later Isabella followed her, in January 1989.

• • •

A 'dead' woman came back to life in the morgue at Glasgow's Royal Infirmary on 3 December 1964. Thirty-five-year-old Catherine Leask was believed to have taken a drug overdose. A spokesman for the hospital said: 'When Mrs Leask first arrived, a physician could detect no trace of life and she was certified dead.' An ambulance man noticed a quiver in her neck as he was about to leave the morgue where Mrs Leask's body had been put when she was pronounced dead. He gave her oxygen and detected a faint pulse. She was quickly removed to intensive care for further treatment and five days later it was announced that she was out of danger.

• • •

JOHN Sinclair of Halkirk, Caithnesss, was married three times, each wife bearing him ten sons. He died in 1890.

• • •

PRIVATE George Mackie's life was saved by divine intervention in 1917 when a German bullet embedded itself in the New Testament Bible he was carrying in the breast pocket of his uniform. Mackie, from Huntly in Aberdeenshire, was with the Gordon Highlanders at the Somme in an area known as Death Valley. The bullet entered the Bible, but only went a quarter of the way in before falling out.

Mackie lived to be ninety-six, dying in 1991, and he treasured the Bible for the rest of his life. In 2000 his family presented the maroon, battle-scarred Bible to the Gordon Highlanders Museum in Aberdeen.

Wondrous Creations

THE Dunmore Pineapple in the grounds of Dunmore Park near Airth in Stirlingshire is an architectural wonder of great beauty. The lower part is a regular Palladian-styled building, but its centrepiece is a work of stunning originality. A small octagonal tower rises from the heart of the building, sprouting spiky leaves, and the structure transforms into a fifty-foot-high pineapple.

It has to be seen to appreciate the stonemason's artistry and skill. Each of the curving stone leaves are drained separately to prevent frost damage to the delicate design. The magnificent folly was built in 1761 on the instructions of John Murray, 4th Earl of Dunmore.

• • •

MEGAN Boyd (1915–2001) from Goldspie, Sutherland, made such perfect flies that fishermen around the world collect them, yet she never caught a fish or ever went fishing.

•   •   •

IN March 1985, the Gleniffer Press of Paisley, Strathclyde, published the world's smallest bound book. It was an edition of the children's story *Old King Cole*, measuring one millimetre by one millimetre, and was printed on twenty-two gsm paper. It could not be read by the naked eye and the pages could be turned only with a needle. Just eighty-five copies were printed. It was verified by the *Guinness Book of Records* as the smallest book in the world and retained that title until an American published a book in 2002 that measured only .9 millimetres by .9 millimetres.

•   •   •

JOHN Stuart McCaig's Folly, inspired by the Colosseum in Rome, dominates the town of Oban in Argyllshire. McCaig was a wealthy banker and decided to build the structure for several reasons. He hoped it would give employment to local crafts people and would also serve as a museum and art gallery. McCaig planned to erect a tower in its centre, which would be decorated with statues of himself and his family.

Work commenced on the huge project in 1897, and over the next five years McCaig spent over £5,000 on the building, but he died in 1902 before it could be completed. At that stage only the outer wall was built and so the construction was abandoned. Instead of the cultural oasis that McCaig had envisaged, the folly now encloses a public garden, with spectacular hillside views of the surrounding countryside.

• • •

WHEN King James I of England (James VI of Scotland) paid a visit to Linlithgow in 1617, he was given a novel welcome by a talking lion. It was a plaster lion, inside of which was concealed the town's schoolmaster, James Wiseman, who greeted the king with a prepared speech.

• • •

THE 'Hundy Mundy' on the Mellerstain Estate near Gordon, Berwickshire, is a wonderful gothic folly which forms a beautiful focal point on the horizon from the front elevation of Mellerstain House. It was built in 1727 by the architect William Adam on the instructions of the estate's owner,

George Baillie. From a distance, it may look like a substantial structure, but it is actually only a wall. Its proper name is Humundas Tower but it is better known by its nickname.

• • •

WHEN Scotsman James Lindsay died in December 1896 in Paterson, New Jersey, he was buried in a coffin he had made years before. Lindsay was a skilled cabinetmaker, but his business had never flourished. He had a little shop on Paterson's Barbour Street for many years. Over the door was a sign that read:

COFFINS MADE AND REPAIRED
Light ones for weavers and strong ones for country folks.

Lindsay made a number of coffins, but no one ever heard of him repairing any. Although poor, Paterson swore he would not be buried in a pauper's box and made his own coffin in preparation for his death. It was made of fine wood and painted with red and white stripes. At the head, inside, Lindsay fixed a photograph of himself and his favourite dog.

The lid had a brass plate with his name inscribed on it. Space was left for the date of his death. The coffin was trimmed inside with wallpaper. Lindsay lived in his little shop and because there was no space for a bed, he used the coffin as one. About a year before his death, poverty forced Lindsay into an almshouse, so he left the coffin in the care of fellow Scotsman John Kidd. When Lindsay died, Kidd had the coffin properly lined with satin, leaving the picture exposed, and buried his friend as he had wished.

• • •

A giant-sized reproduction of Vincent van Gogh's famous painting 'Sunflowers' was created in a field near Duns, Berwickshire in August 1991. A twenty-four-year-old plant nursery manager created the floral masterpiece by using 250,000 flowering plants on a 46,000 square foot section in the heart of a wheatfield. The image was at its best for about a week in mid-August before being ploughed so the land could be returned to agricultural use.

• • •

THE beautiful Royal Arch in Dundee was erected between 1849 and 1853 to commemorate a visit to the city by Queen Victoria and Prince Albert on 11 September 1844. Sadly, this architectural gem was demolished by dynamite on 16 March 1964, to make way for the construction of the Tay Road Bridge.

Stunning Coincidences

A huge wave swept Aberdeen seaman John Craig overboard from the trawler *Dorileen* on 20 November 1956. Minutes later, an equally large wave washed him back on board, while skipper John Watson was out on a lifeboat looking for him.

• • •

AN unusual coincidence occurred during a bridge match in Stirling on 23 October 1945 between the Stirling Club and the 16 Club of Glasgow. When the eighteenth board was dealt, the players discovered that they were holding exactly the same cards as had been dealt them earlier at the second board. After the hand was played, a check of the number two board, which had not been disturbed, confirmed the coincidence. Both hands were dealt from new packs. The odds of this happening are astronomical.

• • •

KATE Jackson from Langley in Northumberland was enjoying a holiday with a friend on the Isle of Mull in the Inner Hebrides in June 2004 when she picked up a battered plastic bottle that had washed up on the beach. When she opened it, she discovered a note inside. The two women were astonished to learn that the note had been written on 23 June 1983 – exactly 21 years to the day before Kate had found it. Amazed by this coincidence, she tracked down the note's author, Max Glaskin, using directory enquiries, and found that he lived in Brighton. Glaskin had holidayed on an island four miles from Mull in 1983 and was delighted to hear that his bottle had been found.

After the story appeared in a Scottish newspaper, the pair were contacted by a researcher from the Jane Pauley Show on NBC Television in America who offered to fly them to New York so that they could meet for the first time on the show. NBC put Kate and Max up in five-star hotels and looked after them well during their stay in New York. They had a wonderful time. 'I still can't believe that NBC flew us over to New York for three days for five minutes on TV,' Kate said. 'It was really incredible. I kept the bottle and took it on to the show, but I think they were quite disappointed with it. It's just an old, dirty and smelly plastic bottle.'

• • •

'MUMMY has done it again,' John Struthers told his children after his wife Janette gave birth to her fifth set of twins in a quarter of a century at Fairfield Hospital in Sydney, Australia on 14 August 1963. A Sydney gynaecologist said that the odds against that many twins being in one family were about 3 billion to 1. The boy and girl, each weighing five pounds, brought the number of children in the Struthers family up to fourteen. Four of their children were born singly. John, Janette and eleven of their children had emigrated from Scotland to Australia in 1961, while their eldest son, James, who was in the British army, remained behind. Forty-four-year-old Janette was quoted as saying, 'It's very exciting news.'

• • •

JOHN Uriasz lost a ring given to him by his late wife while out gardening at his home at Banchory, Kincardineshire, in April 2005. It was returned to him by a magpie. Uriasz's wife Jeanne had given him the golden signet ring on their fiftieth wedding anniversary. It was of enormous sentimental value to the eighty-eight-year-old, whose wife had died five years before. When he realised it was missing, Uriasz searched high and low for the ring, but failed to find it. Two days later he was back in the garden feeding some birds when his ring was returned to him in remarkable circumstances.

'I heard something like a nail landing on concrete,' he recalled. 'A magpie, I think it was one I had been feeding, had dropped something beside me. It was the lost ring. I could not believe it . . . I really believe in miracles now.'

• • •

ANDREW Robert Neil was born in Edinburgh on 11 July 2001 – the same day and month as his father David Neil (34) and his grandfather Robert Lambie (54). The odds of this occurring are said to be 160,000 to one.

• • •

JOHN Culshaw, from Hamilton in Lanarkshire, was fishing on the nearby River Avon on 7 April 1967 when his line hooked a drowning baby. His hook had caught the child's jacket. The child, twenty-month old Sam Rodgers, was floating face down in the water. He had fallen in after wandering way from his riverside home. Sixteen-year-old Culshaw reeled the baby in quickly. At that moment the baby's frantic father came running down the bank and picked up the baby. Newspaper accounts reported that the baby's condition was serious, but that he had a fair chance of surviving.

• • •

TEENAGERS John Johnston and John Barr from Glasgow were each frequently told that they had done things they had not done. After some investigation in 1938, they learned that they were twin brothers. They had not seen each other since they were babies sixteen years before. They had been adopted by different families and were told this when they were old enough, but neither knew he was a twin. The brothers were delighted to be reunited, became firm friends and started a dance band.

• • •

THE Times of 13 September 1848 reprinted a remarkable story from the *Greenock Advertiser*. It details how the captain of a sloop who had lost his keys in Loch Broom in Ross-shire had them returned to him personally, six weeks later and a hundred miles away, while fishing off the island of Raasay. The keys were vomited up by a large cod he had caught. The captain lost his keys when they fell from his pocket into the water in Loch Broom.

His name and the name of his ship were written on a small piece of parchment attached to the keys, and he had given up all hope of ever seeing them again. Amazingly, the fish vomited up his keys, which had the 'partly preserved' parchment attached to prove it.

The article says: 'It is a remarkable circumstance that this fish, in its migratory course, should arrive at the same spot where the sloop was, sacrificing its life, and with its last breath discharging an act of honesty that would have honoured a higher grade of species of animals.' It also coughed up a penknife belonging to another skipper which had his initials engraved on it.

. . .

A gold wedding ring belonging to Mrs William McQueen of Burn House, Lennoxtown, Lanarkshire, was lost in 1916. Twenty-two years later it was found inside a potato dug up from a nearby field. The ring was identified from the name engraved on it and was returned to its owner. Over the twenty-two years, the field had been ploughed and cropped frequently.

. . .

AT 12.50 pm on 23 August 1987, ninety-year-old Grace Jack of Rutherglen died at the Victoria Infirmary in Glasgow. At exactly the same moment, 7.50 am Eastern Standard Time in the United States, her ninety-four-year-old sister Agnes Meike died in a Connecticut nursing home.

. . .

RAY McGurthy from Dundee bought a box of old fishing tackle at an auction in March 1998 and discovered that the contents were wrapped in a newspaper dated 18 September 1944 – the day he was born.

• • •

TWO brothers from Dalkeith in Midlothian met for the first time in May 2001 by pure chance in a Coventry pub. Hugh Monaghan and Patrick McCoole started chatting in the Prince William Henry pub on Foleshill Road when they heard each other's Scottish accents. They soon discovered that they came from the same area and had the same mother! The pair had never met before because Monaghan had been put into care as a baby, long before McCoole was born. Monaghan had settled in Coventry in the 1960s and McCoole had moved there in 1983 to take up a job. More remarkably, both liked to frequent the same pub and lived in the same block of flats on Stoney Stanton Road.

• • •

MRS A.E. Gadsby of Niagara Falls mailed a parcel to her daughter in Prestwick, Ayrshire, in December 1940. The ship carrying the package was torpedoed off the west coast of Ireland, but the tide cast the parcel ashore on the beach at Prestwick. It reached the daughter two days after Christmas.

• • •

ACTRESS Marianne Sellar was playing a vampire at the Edinburgh Dungeon tourist attraction in March 2004 and was about to take a bite from a 'victim' planted in the audience when a visitor told her she had a nosebleed. When Marianne saw the blood, she fainted. Unknown to her bosses, Marianne had a lifelong phobia of blood. 'I had managed to keep my phobia secret for three years because normally we deal only with fake blood, which I can handle,' she said. 'When the visitor showed me all the real blood, I just collapsed.'

Dungeon manager Andrew McDonald said, 'Obviously, we had no idea that our vampire would collapse at the first sight of blood. The visitors got a bit of a fright, but everyone else thinks it is hilarious. It has posed us a problem, though, because we now need to train other actors for the part.' Marianne was given a different job at the dungeon – away from blood.

• • •

WHEN Bob Michie's 1954 R-type Bentley broke down on a remote country road between Fort William and Loch Ailort in October 2005, he feared his car would be off the road for weeks and would be costly to repair. The eighty-seven-year-old had his car towed to a garage and a mechanic discovered that the problem was a broken rotary arm, which provided a spark to the distributor. The garage did not have a spare and had no idea where to get one for the fifty-one-year-old vintage car.

They flagged down a passing AA van and jokingly asked patrolman Mickey Miller if he had one. Amazingly, he did, having kept one in his van for twenty-eight years, 'just in case.' The car was back on the road in minutes. Michie, who was an AA member, could not believe his luck. 'I've known

Mickey for years, but I never knew just what he had in his van.' Miller matter-of-factly said. 'I knew I'd find a use for it some day.'

. . .

MAIRI Hedderwick of Inverness recorded a strange story from her childhood to the *Sunday Mail* in September 1985. When she was a child, her family had lived on the Isle of Coll. Mairi was given a teddy bear when she was a baby. Years later it was put in a skip and dumped at the other end of the island. It washed out to sea. Six months later the teddy bear washed ashore near Mairi's home. She kept it, but later threw it out once more when the family was leaving the island. Two years later they returned on holiday and Mairi found her teddy bear yet again washed ashore on a beach in a poor state.

. . .

THE original Donald Duck was a doctor from Mallaig in Inverness-shire, who was born in 1925, ten years before the popular Walt Disney character, his namesake, was created.

Dr Donald Duck was delighted with his name. On a television programme about people with unusual names, he said: 'I have had so much fun with my name over the years. I wouldn't dream of changing it.' When Duck's canny toy-maker father exhibited some toys, he had a painted sign saying 'painted by Donald Duck'. Lawyers for Walt Disney became involved and Duck's father happily produced his son's birth certificate to prove that he had the name before his cartoon namesake arrived on the scene.

• • •

WHEN two unrelated girls met at Saughton Athletics Club in Edinburgh in the summer of 2002, they found they had a lot in common. Both were called Eilidh Kerr, both were born in Edinburgh on 23 November 1992, and they looked alike. One was born in Eastern General Hospital and the other at Simpson's Maternity. Since both girls had spent the early months of their lives attending the Royal Hospital for Sick Children, their parents were aware of the other Eilidh's existence, but the girls themselves had no knowledge of the other until they met ten years later and became firm friends. When they had attended the same hospital as infants, they left the medical staff so confused that a warning was attached to their medical files to prevent any mix-ups.

• • •

KEN and Liz Roberts from Hilton, Inverness, were on holiday in the small village of Diabaig in Wester Ross in August 1997, strolling along a pier near Loch Diabaig, when they passed by a ringing phone in a public booth. Ken answered it and was flabbergasted to find himself speaking to his mother-in-law Winnie McCracken, who lived in Inverness ninety miles away. She was just as surprised that her son-in-law had answered the lakeside phone.

Mrs McCracken knew that the couple were staying in the area and found the number of a local public phone to try and track them down and so alert Ken to an urgent business problem. 'The phone had been ringing for ages,' Ken explained. 'I was intrigued to find out who would be calling there.' Some of the locals later told the Roberts's that it was the first time the phone box had received a call in years. The phone was the only one within four miles.

•　•　•

AT the battle of Falkirk on 17 January 1746, Major Macdonald, of one of the Macdonald regiments, unhorsed an English officer and immediately mounted the man's very fine horse. When the English cavalry fled, the horse ran away with its captor and, despite all Macdonald's efforts to restrain it, the horse did not stop until it was in the thick of the enemy 'at the head of a regiment of which, apparently, its late master was the commander'. Major Macdonald was captured and hanged – a 'victim of his ambition to possess a fine horse'.

•　•　•

JAMES Maclean from Cromarty looked up just in time on 7 September 1950 to catch a nine-year-old boy as he fell forty feet from a building.

•　•　•

SOME Zulus were on exhibition in 1890s' Aberdeen, and a gentleman who had been in South Africa himself went to see them and got talking to the men in their own language. One of the men was exceptionally shy and the gentleman could make little headway with him. He studied the man closely and recognised the Zulu as someone who had worked for him in Natal and who had run away after stealing a pair of trousers.

• • •

IN December 1950, a surgeon in a Glasgow hospital was about to perform a difficult operation on an elderly patient when he noticed that the man had an extra finger on each hand. (As a young boy, the doctor had been saved from drowning by a fisherman at a fishing port. After pulling the child safely ashore, the man had disappeared. The boy had no clue as to his rescuer's identity, except that the man had an extra digit on each hand.) When the doctor questioned him, the old man replied, 'If I saved your life then, maybe you'll save my life now.' The operation was a success and the old fisherman recovered.

• • •

AN unnamed Scottish couple who bought a 'junk vase' for £1 at a garage sale because they liked the plant growing in it, took the vase along to the *Antiques Roadshow* television programme when it came to Dumfries House, near Cumnock, Ayrshire, in the summer of 2008. It was identified as a rare 1929 glass vase by renowned French designer René Lalique. The couple was stunned, as was antiques expert Eric Knowles when they told him that they had almost thrown out the vase a few days earlier. The couple later sold it for £32,450 at a London auction that November.

• • •

WHEN police issued the description of the body of an unidentified climber that had been found in the Cairngorms on 19 February 1983, Angus and Ethel Clunas of Inverness thought it fitted that of their twenty-four-year-old son Stephen. Along with their son-in-law, Fraser Ross, they went to the morgue and made a formal identification of the body. Ross later said the resemblance to Stephen was 'quite remarkable'. The corpse was wearing the same sweater, parka, underwear and gold watch (with a leather strap) as Stephen.

The family were going through the ordeal of making funeral arrangements when Stephen rang on the day set for his funeral. The mistake had come to light when a friend of Stephen's, who had met him on the day after his 'supposed death', read of his demise in a newspaper and informed the police. When the dead man's fingerprints did not match those taken at Stephen's home, police searched hotels around the area where he was supposed to be staying and found him. He had gone bird-watching and had spent the weekend at the hotel. The identity of the dead man remains a mystery.

• • •

WHILE walking along a riverbank in January 1937, Mr Campbell of Shiel House, Glenshiel, achieved the feat of killing a bird and a fish with one shot. He saw a cormorant swimming sixty yards away from the riverbank and shot it with his rifle. When the bird floated ashore, Campbell examined it. Since the cormorant's neck was quite swollen, Campbell shook the bird and was astonished when it disgorged a grilse weighing just over three pounds. When the cormorant had been killed, the bullet had passed through its body and also through the grilse's body. The bullet hole through the fish could be seen clearly. Campbell sent the cormorant to an Inverness taxidermist.

• • •

ON Christmas Day 1929 there was only one birth at the Edinburgh Royal Maternity and Simpson Memorial Hospital. The mother of the child, a boy, was called Mary and the father was Joseph.

• • •

AT a Perthshire village in September 1911 a Reverend Smith married a Miss Smith to a Mr Smith. Afterwards they set up home in an area where their only neighbours were a Mr and Mrs Smith.

• • •

REVEREND David Lamont (1753–1837) of Kirkpatrick-Durham parish in Dumfriesshire married the girl who was the first infant he ever baptized. She was twenty-one when they married and they lived happily together for thirty-eight years.

• • •

DOREEN Johnson lost her gold signet ring in 1974 while she was playing with her sons in Agnew Park, Stranraer. Her family unsuccessfully searched for it for over a week. Nearly twenty-two years later, her twenty-six-year-old son Robert was working on a project to clean up the park, which had fallen into dereliction, and found the ring while digging. His mother's initials were engraved on its inside, so there was no mistake. The ring had been a gift from Mrs Johnson's grandfather.

• • •

A book borrowed from Inverness Library some time after 1908 was returned to it in September 2004 after being almost 100 years overdue. In the circumstances, the library waived the £5,000 fine the book had racked up. The book, *Inverness Sketches 1901 to 1904* by Isabel Harriet Anderson, was bought by Inverness man Stuart Thomson at a flea market in Johannesburg.

'I just looked at the book and saw Inverness on it and thought hell, I've just got to buy this book,' he recalled. When Thomson moved back to Scotland in 2004, he remembered the book and thought he should bring it home. The book had Inverness Public Library printed on it and Thomson presented it to the library on his return to his native town. It had originally been presented to the library by its author and should not have been loaned out in the first place. Just how it ended up in South Africa remains a mystery.

• • •

ACCORDING to the *Lochaber News* of 16 September 2000, fragments of glass rained down on the congregation at a church in Fort William when a light exploded as the choir finished a hymn with the words 'nothing can our peace destroy'.

• • •

LINDA Riley from Newburgh, who worked as an insurance underwriter, won compensation after she tripped and fell over a pile of accident claim forms at her work in Perth on 13 August 2002.

On 25 January 2006, Ms Riley reached an out-of-court settlement with her employer, Norwich Union. As a result of the accident, she was left with pain in her left ankle, lower leg and was still suffering from pain three years after the accident. Not only this, she was absent from work for a period and lost wages as a result. The out-of-court settlement was reached after she had taken Norwich Union to court, seeking £5,000 as compensation for the loss and injury she had suffered as a result of the accident.

• • •

JANE Burgess was astonished to learn that the doctor who was going to deliver her baby in New York was the same doctor who had brought her into the world 34 years before. She was born in Aberdeen Maternity Hospital in 1968 and delivered by Dr Anthony Lopes. After she married, she moved to New York, and it was there she became pregnant.

While searching online for a doctor to carry out the birth of her baby, Jane picked Dr Lopes after noticing that he had worked in Aberdeen. She made contact and during their conversation Dr Lopes said he had been in Aberdeen at the time and suggested that he may have helped to deliver Jane. She checked with her mother, Janet Patterson, who thought his name rang a bell. She checked Jane's baby book and confirmed that it had been Dr Lopes.

Not only that: Jane was close to death with breathing difficulties when she was born and Dr Lopes had revived her. Dr Lopes moved to America and fate brought them together again. In March 2002, he delivered Jane's baby son James. 'It was very special having Dr Lopes deliver James,' she said.

• • •

A giant wave helped to save nine Germans clinging to the keel of their overturned ship in the raging north Atlantic seas off Aberdeen on 29 January 1956. It washed them clear of the suction area as their vessel, the *Gertrod*, sank. Nearby trawlers picked up all nine sailors.

• • •

GLASGOW insurance salesman Ronald Myall made an embarrassing disclosure in court in January 1963 while testifying against four men charged with robbing his home. When Myall sheepishly admitted that he was not insured at the time of the theft, the court erupted in laughter. Myall added that he was currently insured.

• • •

WHILE playing 'I Spy' with her parents during a car journey on 15 April 2002, seven-year-old Nicole Lovie spotted smoke coming from an apartment building in Edinburgh. The Lovies raised the alarm, called the fire service and probably saved lives. The Lovies from Restalrig were on their way to buy dinner when Nicole spotted the smoke rising from the Rossie Place flats off Easter Road.

'Nicole started to get very excited, saying she saw smoke coming from a building,' her mother Debbie explained. 'Her father, James, told her not to be silly but she persisted, saying, "Please, Daddy, go back. I saw smoke." She said it about three times and was getting more and more upset before my husband decided to humour her. It was about 10pm and she was tired, so we thought she was just imagining it.'

• • •

THE bride wore white, the groom and the best man wore big red noses, and nobody batted an eyelid when Peewee the clown married his bride in style on 12 January 1989. Peewee – twenty-year-old Stuart Bailey of the Barnum & Bailey circus dynasty – married animal superintendent Christine Gourlay in true circus tradition, in the sawdust ring where their circus was performing in Edinburgh.

• • •

ACCORDING to the book *Ripley's Believe It or Not! Strange Coincidences* (1990), David Lawson Kerr of Stirling wrote his name and address on a piece of paper and securely placed it inside a watertight bottle. He threw the bottle into the sea off the Gambian coast in West Africa. Eight months later it washed ashore over 3,000 miles away on Fowl Bay beach, St. Philip, Barbados where it was found by David Lawson of Bethesda, Maryland.

Unlucky Occurrences

DAVID Leggat was trapped inside a toilet for four days in December 2007. The fifty-five-year-old Leggat was locked inside the gents' toilets of Kittybrewster and Woodside bowling club in Aberdeen. He endured the ordeal with fortitude. He was by himself locking up the clubhouse on the evening of 3 December when he nipped into the toilet before leaving, without bothering to turn on the lights. When the door closed behind him, the handle fell off on the other side and he could not reopen the door.

Leggat instantly knew he was in for a long wait because the club was used infrequently at that time of year. It would be three days later before the club secretary, Bob Ewing, dropped by the clubhouse to check if it was in order, but he did not hear Leggat's cries for help from the back of the building. The following day, cleaner Cathy Scollay arrived at the clubhouse and heard Leggat shouting for help. She could not open the door but rang Ewing for help and they were able to free Leggat at last.

Leggat was wearing only light clothes when he was snared in the dark toilets and had no mobile phone to call for help. The first night was very cold and he could not get comfortable enough to sleep in the cramped, tiled space. His only means of staying warm was to keeping running a basin of hot water and putting his feet in to send the heat through his body. He had no food to eat and he sipped on cold tap water to keep going. It was only during the short hours of daylight that the sun shone into the room through a skylight high in the roof.

• • •

IN January 2000, a terrified Belgian tourist returned a two pound stone he had taken from an ancient burial site as a memento because he believed his family had been cursed since he had appropriated it. The man claimed that since he had taken the stone, his daughter had broken a leg, his wife had become ill, and he had lost his job. The Belgian was convinced that he had been cursed and posted the stone to the Inverness Tourist Information Centre, begging them to return it to its rightful spot at Clava Cairns near Culloden in an anonymous letter.

'He understood it all sounded a bit strange, but he had traced the family's bad luck back to when he took the stone,' said Bob Hunter-Dorens of the tourist centre, adding, 'He was most anxious we took it back to the exact spot he found it.'

• • •

THE heavy hand of fate dealt a blow to Glasgow man Leonard McCallum in May 1963. After finishing a cigarette, McCallum flicked the butt out of his car window while driving. The wind caught the cigarette and blew it back into the car and up one of McCallum's sleeves. While frantically trying to shake out the cigarette, he lost control of his car. It mounted a pavement and got jammed between a lamp-post and the parapet of a bridge. Luckily, no other drivers or pedestrians were harmed and McCallum escaped with minor injuries.

• • •

CROSS Kirk Graveyard at Eshaness in the Shetland Islands has one of the most curious tombstone inscriptions to be found anywhere:

Donald Robertson, born 4 January 1783.
Died June 1842. Aged 63 years.
He was a peaceable quiet man, and, to all appearance,
a sincere Christian.
His death was much regretted which was caused by
the stupidity of Laurence Tulloch in Clothister (Sollum)
who sold him nitre instead of Epsom Salts, by which
he was killed in the space of 5 hours after taking a dose of it.

Tulloch moved away to Aberdeen where he opened a shop in 1852.

• • •

THE Scotsman of 16 August 1990 details the misadventures of a Yorkshire policeman who had arrested three Scotsmen suspected of car theft and other crimes. Constable Malcolm Hodgson helped arrest the three men. He then made the trip to Kirkcaldy, Fife, in January 1990 to give evidence at their trial, only to be told that the trial had been postponed and that he had made the 600-mile round trip for nothing. At a later date, Constable Hodgson was preparing to leave for his holidays in Switzerland when he learned that he had to attend the trial on a date that was in the middle of his break.

Hodgson borrowed £450 and flew to Scotland where he was once again told the trial had been moved to a future date. Fortunately, he was allowed to give evidence at a special sitting, then he flew back to Switzerland to resume his holiday, only to learn that his luggage had ended up in Hamburg, where police thought the unattended luggage suspicious, mistook it for a bomb and blew it up.

• • •

HISTORIAN Thomas Carlyle (1795–1881) from Ecclefechan, Dumfriesshire, had spent nearly a year working on the first volume of his epic *History of the French Revolution*. He sent the completed manuscript to a friend, fellow writer John Stuart Mill, for his opinion. Mill judged it to be a work of genius and stayed up late reading it into the small hours before heading for bed, leaving the manuscript in an untidy pile on his desk. The next morning (6 March 1835) Mill's maid mistook the pages for waste paper and used Carlyle's precious work to light a fire.

When Carlyle learned the fate of his manuscript, he was beside himself with grief. Frantically, he set about rewriting the manuscript, but this only made him feel worse and he failed in his task. He rested and did nothing but read novels for several weeks, then threw himself back into his work with gusto and rewrote the entire manuscript. The completed three-volume work was published in 1837 and was an immediate critical and financial success.

• • •

ON 15 June 1983, an RAF rescue helicopter searched the Firth of Clyde, and all vessels in the area were alerted to help find the source of an activated distress beacon. It was only after an extensive air-sea search failed to find any sailors in trouble that the source of the distress signal was traced to a house in Erskine, Strathclyde, where a faulty beacon was lying on the top of a wardrobe in the bedroom of Mr and Mrs Leslie Brown. While they were sleeping, it started to broadcast and the signal was picked up by a Soviet satellite and relayed to the RAF.

Newspapers at the time said the Brown had bought the distress beacon for their sailing boat. The following March, a different story emerged when Brown was prosecuted for stealing the pocket-sized beacon from an oilrig where he had worked.

• • •

AN unnamed physical education teacher suffered from frostbite when she fell asleep, leaving a bag of frozen chips on an injured foot for at least forty minutes in 2000. Her foot became sore and discoloured and she lost feeling in her toes. The forty-two-year-old woman was sent to Crosshouse Hospital in Kilmarnock where she was treated for third-degree frostbite. She needed surgery to remove the damaged tissue and underwent a skin graft. She was left with permanent damage to her two toes. Experts recommend that ice packs be used only for a short period with a damp towel placed between the pack and the skin.

• • •

A Fort William man made a 550-mile trip in April 2008 to buy a particular model of car he had set his heart on, only to discover that it was the same car he had been admiring in his home town for weeks. Jamie Ball went to inspect an Alfa Romeo in a Bristol dealership and discovered it was the same car he had seen in a car park back in Scotland. He was astonished to learn that it had previously been owned by a friend of his, John Harvey. Harvey had traded in the car for a Subaru Outback at the Bristol dealership, which informed him that they had two enquiries about the car from his own area. One was from a person in Ballachulish, Argyllshire, and the other was from Ball, who thus bought the car knowing he could have saved himself over a thousand-mile journey and about the same amount in money if he had left a note on the car's windscreen when he had first seen it.

• • •

A Royal Navy frigate fired on a beach off Cape Wrath, Sutherland, on 21 July 1968 and hit a housewife who was out collecting shells. Forty-five-year-old Nellie Munro was struck on the legs and thighs by fragments from the shell. She was taken to a warship in the area for treatment. The Royal Navy made a full apology to Mrs Munro and said that it was investigating the incident. The frigate was on naval exercises in the waters off the Cape.

Medical Marvels

GLASGOW man Pat Mulloy lost his bottom set of false teeth in 1960. Four years later the seventy-four-year-old found them again – in his throat! They had been stuck there since he had swallowed them in his sleep. The dentures were retrieved by doctors at the Western Infirmary where Mulloy went for an operation on his hand. The blockage in his throat was discovered while he was being prepared for the anaesthetic. 'My top set got broken,' Mulloy said. 'My bottom set vanished mysteriously just about four years ago. I can't remember swallowing them. I woke up one morning and they were gone.'

• • •

JUST before the start of the summer holidays in 1989, six-year-old Sarah Jayne Tait from Edinburgh came home upset and crying because she had a swollen and painful left eye. Her family and doctor could see nothing in the eye, but an eye specialist put a probe round behind it and out popped a baked bean. Sarah Jayne had no idea how it had got there – she did not even like baked beans.

• • •

CORMACK'S *Edinburgh Medical Journal* of 1844 contains an account of a thirty-one-year-old Leith man whose death was caused by a potato skin. The man died from asphyxiation. An autopsy discovered a triangular piece of potato skin, little more than an inch long, lodged in his larynx. It was as transparent and thin as a piece of paper and formed a valve that would open at each expiration, but shut at each inhalation, thereby quickly suffocating the man. The man had died while in a state of intoxication and the potato skin had probably been ejected from his stomach by vomiting and had accidentally become lodged in his throat.

• • •

SURGEONS at the Royal Infirmary in Edinburgh were called to an unusual case on 23 March 1837. Five weeks before, a woman, fooling about with friends, accidentally swallowed a small brass padlock. It was one and two-thirds inches long, was over an inch wide and weighed nearly an ounce. The padlock lodged in her throat and was extremely painful. She took an emetic, but this failed to dislodge the padlock. For the first twenty-four hours, the unfortunate woman was in a great deal of pain and felt as if she was suffocating.

After that first day, she felt no pain and did nothing about it until 19 March. She was admitted to the hospital under the care of Professor Lizars, who believed her story. Other professors doubted her explanation and nothing was done immediately to remove the lock. When violent vomiting, pain and a sense that the patient was suffocating returned late one night, Professor Lizars' hospital assistant, Dr James Johnson, rushed to the woman's aid. Seeing that the woman would soon die if the padlock was not removed, he extracted it from her throat with the aid of a specially designed surgical instrument. The woman recovered.

• • •

ROBERT Naysmith from Montrose in Angus was known as the human ostrich. He spent ten years travelling around Britain as a sideshow freak, swallowing nails, glass, ladies' hatpins, tacks, needles, stones and other sundry items. He sickened and died in a London hospital in 1906. The post mortem revealed that he had 'swallowed too many indigestible items'. More than thirty nails and hatpins were found in his kidneys and liver, but mostly in his intestines.

• • •

ACCORDING to the *Guinness Book of Records 1989*, the longest period spent without solid food was 382 days when Angus Barbieri lived on tea, coffee, water, soda water and vitamins in Mary Field Hospital, Dundee, in the mid-1960s. The twenty-six-year-old from Tay Port, Fife weighed thirty-three stone, ten pounds and had gone to Mary Field Hospital the previous year to seek help in losing weight. He was advised to stop eating. After his fast, Barbieri's weight was down by more than twenty stone to a mere twelve stone, eleven pounds. When he tried on his old clothes, another two people could get into his suit beside him. Two weeks before he started eating again, doctors put him on a salt diet. The following week he was given sugar, and then on 11 July 1966 his first meal in 382 days was put before him.

• • •

A pin lodged in a Glasgow woman's lung for ten years was successfully extracted during an operation performed at the Glasgow Royal Infirmary on 19 December 1927. Repeated efforts had been made over the years, without success, to remove the pin, and the woman had become weaker and thinner, until her life was despaired of. The operation came about because a doctor had taken an interest in the case, and after an X-ray examination of the woman's lung, he had recovered the pin.

• • •

SURGEONS at the Dundee Royal Infirmary successfully sewed a three-year-old girl's lip back on after a vet had removed it from the stomach of the dog that had bitten it off. Megan MacFarlane from Arbroath was eating an ice cream on 10 July 1997 when the 100 lb bull mastiff jumped up and bit her face. Paramedics called to the scene could not find her top lip and guessed that the dog must have swallowed it. With the owner's permission, a vet put down the dog, then cut open its stomach and extracted the child's lip.

It was put in a mixture of saline and ice to preserve it and police rushed it the 15 miles to the hospital where Megan was being treated. The plastic surgeon who carried out the operation said that it was the first time he knew of that human tissue had been reattached after being recovered from the stomach of an animal. 'The dog had not chewed the lip; otherwise, the operation would have been impossible, although the edges were a bit crushed,' said Dr Anas Naasan.

Fortunately, the lip had not been inside the dog long enough to be damaged by stomach acid.

• • •

THE existence of horned humans is a verified medical oddity. There are numerous medically accepted cases of these unusual phenomena. In the past, many museums had specimens of these horns preserved in their collections, but most have been lost through careless or deliberate action. Scotland's own horned celebrity was Elizabeth Lowe. On 14 May 1671, when Lowe was fifty years old, surgeon Arthur Temple cut off a 4½-inch horn from her skull, in front of

witnesses. The horn had been growing from an area three inches above her right ear for seven years before its surgical removal. By 1682 it was recorded that another horn had grown from the same spot on her head. Shaped like a stretched out letter 'S', the hard, dark, brown horn was carefully preserved in the Anatomical Museum of Edinburgh for many years. Unlike many other specimens, it still exists and is now in the Anatomical Collections of the Department of Biomedical Science, University of Edinburgh Medical School.

•   •   •

IN their book *Anomalies and Curiosities of Medicine*, doctors Gould and Pyle tell of a six-year-old Zulu boy who was exhibited in Edinburgh in 1882. Anyone touching him received a mild electric shock. He had displayed this unusual phenomenon from infancy. Shaking hands with the boy gave one a mild 'quivering sensation like that produced by an electric current'. Contact with his tongue resulted in a sharper shock.

•   •   •

GLASGOW-born Jennifer Quigley (1851–1936) was known as the 'Scottish Queen' throughout her fifty-year stage career. The nickname was given to her by the great showman P.T. Barnum when she arrived in America at the age of thirteen. There are varying descriptions of her size. One says she was twenty-eight inches tall and weighed thirty-two pounds but her obituary published in several American newspapers in March 1936 says that she was forty-one inches tall. Whatever size Jennifer Quigley was, all agree that she was a highly skilled performer and travelled the globe entertaining royalty and lesser folk with her acting and singing. Sometimes she was given starring roles, but she would frequently perform during the intermission to entertain the audience until the main act resumed.

One historian says that whenever Jennifer could, she would make a grand entrance on stage in a miniature carriage pulled by a Shetland pony. A splendidly liveried coachman would open the door, 'bow with reverence, and assist Jennie as she regally stepped down to the stage floor'. After half a century travelling the world, Jennifer Quigley retired from the stage in 1917 and died at her nephew's home in Chicago nearly twenty years later.

• • •

JOHN Maceachin, a seventy-five-year-old labourer from Argyle, broke his thigh in 1921 and was taken to the West Highland Rest Hospital in Oban. After a meal, he fell asleep, and until he died fifteen years later, he slept for twenty-two hours a day. He awoke for meals, but never spoke a word again.

• • •

THE *Gentleman's Magazine* of 1736 contains the following strange entry for 3 January: 'One David Ferne was brought to town, born in the Shire of Ross in Scotland, aged twenty-six, but thirty inches high and thirty-five round. All his features human, but his hands resembled the feet of a seal, and his feet those of a bear.'

• • •

DR Dyce of Aberdeen chronicled the unusual case of a sixteen-year-old girl who would suddenly fall asleep in the daytime and then would begin sleep-talking and continue doing household tasks. When she awoke, she would have no knowledge of what she had done while in that state. Dr Dyce recorded that this had occurred from 2 March to 11 June 1815. On one occasion the girl imagined that she was a Church of England clergyman and carried out a baptismal service for three children, intoning the appropriate prayers. Sometimes she would answer questions and undertake her usual tasks as a maid while asleep. She was known to lay the table for breakfast and dress herself and the children while fast asleep.

On one occasion she walked to church with her employer while asleep, attended the service and appeared as devoted as any other churchgoer. She became so touched by the sermon that tears rolled down her cheeks. When awake, she had no memory of this, but the next time this condition occurred, the girl answered questions about the sermon and repeated passages from it. She told Dr Dyce that she knew these sleeping fits were coming on when her sight grew dim and she felt a strange noise in her head. Dr Dyce himself witnessed her sleepwalking state and watched her read out loud from a book and sing a hymn. He observed that her eyes were usually half-closed and her pupils dilated. Dr Dyce could provide no explanation for this extraordinary phenomenon.

• • •

IN rare cases, some people have displayed the ability to control their heartbeat. In his 1845 book *The Philosophy of Mystery*, Walter Cooper Dendy includes a brief description of a case witnessed by Dr Cleghorn of Glasgow some decades before. Dr Cleghorn attended a man who could pretend to be dead and had the ability to control his heart at will and lower his heartbeat so much that a pulse could not be felt. Some years afterwards the man died suddenly – and this time permanently.

• • •

THE *Sunday Mail* of 11 June 1989 reported a miraculous case of a blind man regaining his sight. Glasgow man Maurice Elder had lost his sight because of diabetes. Treatments to try and restore his vision had failed. Eye specialists told the fifty-three-year-old that the chances of him ever seeing again were slim. In May 1989, Elder was sleeping in an armchair at his home in Shawlands when he was awoken by a loud bang outside his window. He was so startled that he jumped to his feet and found that he could see again.

• • •

MRS James Brekenridge from Hamilton, Ontario, Canada, was able to speak in December 1956 after being voiceless for twenty-nine years. She had swallowed a chicken bone and doctors removing it found what other physicians had searched for for years before without any success – a displaced vocal chord. They were able to operate and repair the vocal chord, thus allowing her to speak again. Mrs. Brekenridge emigrated to Canada from Scotland when she was seventeen and spoke with a Scottish accent after the operation that restored her speech.

• • •

IN *Anomalies and Curiosities of Medicine*, Gould and Pyle report the case of a teenage girl who was in an asylum in Edinburgh during the nineteenth century. When she became excited, her normally blonde hair turned red over a period of two or three days. It remained that way for seven or eight days before it reverted to its natural blonde state.

• • •

REGGIE Myles from Tullibody, Clackmannanshire, suffered from a rare disease in 2006 and unexpectedly discovered that a side-effect of his treatment made him look twenty years younger. Sixty-two-year-old Myles was struck down by the genetic disorder *porphyria cutanea tarda*, and his full head of grey hair fell out. His weight plummeted from 230 pounds (104 kilograms) to just ninety-eight pounds (forty-four kilograms) and even the simplest tasks, such as making a cup of tea, became impossible. He was put on a tough range of treatments, which included taking steroids and undergoing radiation therapy. As a side-effect of this, Myles and his doctors were shocked when his hair grew back dark brown and many of his wrinkles disappeared. His altered appearance meant that he was often mistaken for his sons, then in their forties.

• • •

SARAH Sutherland from Falkirk woke up on 22 May 1962 and could hear again after a dream. The forty-two-year-old had been deaf since birth. 'It was just an ordinary dream,' she said. 'I dreamed I was talking to someone and then I woke up, and I could hear sounds in the house. I do not know what happened. I cannot explain it.'

• • •

WHILE working as a surgeon in Calcutta, Dr James Esdaile (1808–59) from Montrose successfully performed more than 2,000 operations on patients who had been hypnotised. The patients felt no pain and death rates, which had been around fifty percent, fell to five percent. He also discovered the level of hypnosis at which natural anaesthesia occurs and it was named the Esdaile state in his honour. The use of anaesthetics soon overshadowed Esdaile's work.

• • •

IN his book *The Code of Health and Longevity* (1807), Sir John Sinclair includes the remarkable case of Patrick Machell Vivan, who was born in Whithorn, Galloway in 1546 and who lived to be 111. He became a clergyman and ministered at Lesbury near Alnwick in Northumberland for the final half of his life.

What was most remarkable and attested to by several people was that when Vivan was about 110, his sight vastly improved. At the age of seventy, he could not read even the largest print without glasses. At the end of his life, Vivan found he could read the smallest print or writing without them.

Three new teeth started to grow again when he was 109; this was a painful experience. He had been bald, but by the time a writer named Thomas Aitken met him in October 1657, Vivan had a head of 'flaxen' hair like a child's. The venerable old clergyman was still ministering at that time and preached an hour-and-a-half sermon on the day that Aitken visited. Not long before that, the clergyman had walked to Alnwick and back from his home. He also married again and had five more children when he was over 80 years old.

•   •   •

IN the eighteenth century, Dr F.W. Cumming left £600 to the Royal Infirmary in Edinburgh to provide poor patients, of both sexes, with snuff and tobacco. He gave the following reason for this unusual bequest: 'I know how to feel for the suffering of those, who in addition to the irksomeness of pain and the tedium of confinement, have to endure the privation of what long habit has rendered in a great degree a necessity of life.'

•   •   •

NAOMI Easton was nearly killed when a seven-foot long plank of wood fell on her on 17 April 2009, driving two nails into her skull. The eleven-year-old was impaled when the plank fell as she was helping to build a hut with friends near her home in Pumpherston, West Lothian. At first, Naomi thought she had a twig tangled in her hair. 'When I went to pull it out, it was stuck. That's when I started screaming. We didn't know there were nails in it,' she said. 'Some of the people that were there went to get their mums. Then the ambulance came and that was it. It was quite painful. Today,

I feel a little bit sore, but I'm just glad that I'm still here and I've got my mum.'

Medics were unable to get Naomi into an ambulance initially because the plank was too long, so firefighters had to trim it before the brave girl could fit inside the ambulance. 'When I got to where Naomi was lying, I was frozen,' her mother Lynette said. 'She was sitting under a tree saying, "Sorry mum." Doctors told me Naomi avoided death because one of the nails was bent, causing it to miss her brain by a few millimetres.' Naomi went on to make a perfect recovery.

• • •

CZECH speedway driver Matej Kus was involved in a terrible accident at a Glasgow track on 9 September 2007. He crashed and was thrown over his bike's handlebars. Another rider unavoidably ran over his head, splitting Kus's helmet. The seventeen-year-old lay unconscious on the track for nearly an hour before coming to. He had flown into Britain just the previous day and knew only the most basic English phrases, but when he regained consciousness he spoke fluent English to the paramedics and even had an English accent. 'I couldn't believe what I was hearing,' said Peter Waite, the promoter of Kus's team, the Berwick Bandits. 'He had changed from someone I could hardly understand to someone who sounded like a BBC announcer. Whatever happened in the crash must have rearranged things in his head.'

Kus said he did not know who or where he was or even his nationality. He had injured ligaments in his left knee and was told to take it easy for a month. His new-found fluency in English soon faded away. After flying home to Plzen in the Czech Republic, Kus said through an interpreter that he had no memory of the accident or the following two days. 'I hope I can pick English up over the winter, for the start of the next season, so that I'll be able to speak it without someone having to hit me over the head first.'

One explanation for Kus's ability to speak a foreign language without learning it is that the head injury had removed his inhibitions to speak English. He had had lessons in school, which must have stayed in his subconscious.

• • •

PEEBLES-born brothers William and Robert Chambers were hugely successful publishers in the nineteenth century. Their most famous work, *Chambers Dictionary*, first published in 1871, remains in print. Unusually, the brothers were both born with six fingers on each hand and six toes on each foot. Popular belief held at the time was that this was very lucky, but the boys' parents decided otherwise and their sons had to undergo operations to remove the supernumerary fingers and toes. William's were removed successfully, but Robert's toes were so badly amputated that he was left partly lame.

• • •

A mysterious case of human combustion (although not spontaneous) was reported by a Dr De Brus in the March 1829 edition of the *Edinburgh Medical and Surgical Journal*. A man's hands had burst into bright blue flames when he tried to help his brother whose clothes had caught fire. His hands burned for several hours with a flickering blue flame, which was finally extinguished after he had kept them immersed in water for a long period.

• • •

WHEN eighteen-year-old Donovan McGowan from Glasgow underwent an operation at the city's Southern General Hospital after being hit by a car in March 2008, surgeons accidentally left behind a four-inch-long metal bar inside his head. It was discovered when McGowan demanded a scan after suffering from agonizing headaches and swelling on the side of his head over a three-month period.

• • •

DOCTORS found a two-inch needle embedded in Christine Macleod's chest after she set off a security metal detector at Stornoway airport in the Isle of Lewis in July 1997. Despite the fact that she was carrying nothing metallic, the alarm at the security gate went off. She had recently suffered from chest pains, and noticed a long thin lump on her body only when she checked. Christine immediately went to doctors in Stornoway, who sent her to Raigmore Hospital in Inverness for further tests.

A mammogram clearly showed a needle inside Christine's right breast. 'I was startled, horrified and speechless when I saw the X-ray,' she said. 'The radiographer and consultant said they had never seen anything like it. You could even see the eye of this two-inch needle. It was pointing upwards. My immediate worry was that it would pierce my heart.' Christine believed it must have entered her body when she was sewing.

She flew home to Cearn Fhlodaidh on the Isle of Lewis and, a few weeks later, successfully underwent surgery to remove the needle.

• • •

THE *Glasgow Medical Journal* of 1859 contains an account of a baker's daughter who was able to remain in an oven at 274 degrees Fahrenheit for twelve minutes and was apparently unaffected by the temperature.

• • •

ROBERT Wood from Glenrothes, Fife, cooked in his sleep. As often as five times a week, he climbed out of his bed, went down to his kitchen, cooked food and performed other household tasks. Usually he prepared snacks of chips, omelettes and stir fries. He even made spaghetti bolognaise with his own special sauce. Sometimes he set the table, turned on the television or ran a bath.

His night-time culinary activities terrified Wood and his wife Eleanor, who were afraid that some day he would accidentally set the house on fire. Fifty-five-year-old Wood started sleepwalking as a fourteen-year-old, but the problem wasn't realised until he married in 1992 and Eleanor learned the danger his sleepwalking presented. As of March 2006, Wood was being treated at the Edinburgh Sleep Centre.

• • •

ACCORDING to the *Guinness Book of Records*, the tallest Scotsman and the tallest 'true' giant (with no growth abnormalities) was Angus MacAskill (1825–63) from the isle of Berneray in the Outer Hebrides. MacAskill measured seven feet nine inches and was famous for his feats of strength. He reputedly once lifted a ship's anchor weighing 2,800 pounds to chest height and he even lifted a hundred pound weight (fifty kilograms) with two fingers and held it at arms length for ten minutes. It was little wonder that he entered show business and travelled throughout Europe and North America with P.T. Barnum's circus. The MacAskill family had immigrated to Cape Breton Island in Nova Scotia when Angus was a child and he eventually returned there and invested his earnings in property and businesses.

• • •

LEIGH Robertson from Aberdeen was born with fused fingers on both her hands, and an underdeveloped right leg with a clubfoot. In July 1979, surgeons at the Royal Aberdeen Children's Hospital decided to replace her right leg with an artificial limb and give the brave four-year-old a pair of thumbs constructed from three of the toes from the amputated limb. In a successful operation, a right-hand thumb was made from a big toe and two other toes were fused to make a left thumb. Surgeons took the bandages off her hands on 6 August and reported the operation a success.

• • •

ON 20 August 1771 a man from Irvine, Ayrshire, was struck by lightning and regained his hearing after being deaf for 20 years.

• • •

EDINBURGH man Sir James Young Simpson (1811–70) was a doctor and an important figure in medical history. Simpson discovered the anaesthetic properties of chloroform and successfully introduced it to medical usage. Before anaesthetics became commonplace, the patient was always fully awake while under a doctor's knife. In 1846, Simpson learned of the newly discovered use of ether as an anaesthetic in America and decided to experiment with medical colleagues using various 'noxious vapours' to discover a better anaesthetic.

After several evenings of experiments, the breakthrough came on 4 November 1847 at Simpson's home in Queen Street when he and his colleagues lost consciousness after taking a sniff of chloroform – much to the alarm of the ladies present at the dinner party. When Simpson came around, he realised he had found a better and stronger anaesthetic than ether. Four days later, Simpson made medical history when, in delivering Wilhelmina Carstairs, he became the first person to use anaesthesia in childbirth and chloroform in clinical practice.

• • •

STEVIE Starr from Glasgow is a professional regurgitator and has performed across the world and on many television shows. He can swallow objects such as rings, lightbulbs, balloons, billiard balls, nails, dry sugar and goldfish and regurgitate them with no harm to himself (or the goldfish). Amazingly, Starr can retrieve objects at will in whichever order is requested. His astonishing act never fails to amaze audiences.

• • •

AFTER being blind for two-and-a-half years, a miner regained his sight while lying in bed in an Edinburgh hospital in August 1956 where he had been detained for observation after complaining of headaches. Forty-three-year-old Robert McKechnie from Broxburn, Lothian, cancelled an application for admission to the Edinburgh Royal Blind Asylum as a basket worker and reported to the local labour exchange in the hope of finding a job. The father of seven had been diagnosed as suffering from miners' nystagmus. Speaking to reporters, he described the sensation of seeing again: 'I thought I saw a tree out of the window. I got out of bed and saw not only a tree but the hills beyond.' McKechnie was allowed home and saw his two youngest children for the first time.

• • •

THOMAS Gordon was an unusual centenarian. At the age of 100 his snow-white hair suddenly changed to jet-black. In the same year, Gordon passed a driving test so well that officials said many younger applicants could envy his eyesight. Gordon claimed that, in four generations of his family, only one natural death had occurred under the age of 101 and that person was ninety-three. He was born in Scotland in 1829 and emigrated to Boston with his family two years later. Gordon settled in Michigan in 1852 and never failed to vote in a presidential election, except in 1862 when he was at sea as a sailor. He celebrated his 104th birthday on 23 September 1933.

• • •

TWENTY-one-year-old John Gray was blinded in one eye during a German air raid on Glasgow in 1941. When he started to go blind in his good eye in 2007, at the age of eighty-seven, eye specialists decided to see if they could restore the sight to the eye that had been damaged sixty-six years before. The retina in Gray's blind eye was perfect, but the lens was badly damaged. In a risky operation at the Southern General Hospital, eye surgeon Dr Ian Bryce removed the scared lens and replaced it with a new artificial lens – something possible only because of advances in medical technology. It took several weeks for Gray's brain to readjust to using the eye again but, amazingly, the sight slowly returned and by April 2008, the vision in this eye was good enough to allow him to read small print.

Entertaining Accidents

THE mate of the Aberdeen trawler *Avonside*, who was said to be no more superstitious than any sailor, had the fright of his life one night in October 1932 when, sixty miles off the Scottish coast, he saw a hazy figure climb over the stern on to the ship from the open sea and disappear into the shadows forward. He called the captain and they both investigated. The moonlight night showed up a trail of wet footprints leading to the crew's quarters.

Inside, a pile of wet clothing lay on the floor. Nearby, sailor Alfred Middleton lay shivering in his bunk. He explained that he had walked overboard in his sleep. The shock of the cold North Sea brine had woken him and he had had the instinct to grab a rope as the stern went slipping by. Feeling embarrassed, Middleton had crept back to his bunk, hoping that he would not be noticed.

●　●　●

A truck carrying 4,200 bottles of gin collided with a car owned by a rival gin company at Leith in October 1960. Not a single bottle of gin was broken.

• • •

DURING a performance at the Edinburgh Festival on 7 September 1961, the shorts of one of the army's kilted Highland Dancers fell down in front of an audience of 7,000 people. The hugely embarrassed soldier was dancing with his fellow Highlanders when the elastic on his shorts broke and they fell to his ankles. The accident almost stopped his show, but the soldier retained his sang froid, stepping out of the shorts and dancing out of the spotlight's arms while clutching his kilt. An army spokesman was only prepared to say that 'the soldier dealt with the situation in a proper military manner'. Another army spokesman said, 'Of course, the Highlanders don't normally wear shorts under their kilt. Only for dancing, you know.'

• • •

WHEN Alison McKenzie from Peterhead, Aberdeenshire, rang an environmental twenty-four-hour help line, run by Aberdeenshire Council in May 2000, to complain about a 'green' chorizo sausage she had bought from her local Safeway supermarket, she was unprepared for the response. A glitch in a British Telecom computer system put her message on the major incident voice bank of most British police forces. It was sent to every BT pager in Britain beginning with the number 01426. Soon Alison was inundated with calls from police, doctors, nurses, careers and business people from all over the country. British Telecom had to bring in engineers to erase the message from their system.

• • •

IN May 1960, an Edinburgh jury rejected a fifty-two-year-old Frenchwoman's claim for damages for injuries she said she had suffered when 'she was ambushed' by a lion skin rug in a hotel in the Scottish capital. The jury decided that Mrs Rolande Neff should have been looking where she was going when she walked into the manager's office of the Golden Lion Hotel three years previously. Mrs Neff claimed that she had stumbled over the lion rug's nine-inch head and had fractured a shoulder, which doctors told her would never be the same again. She was looking for £1,750 in damages from the hotel's owners.

The accident happened when Mrs Neff was on vacation in Scotland. Defence witnesses said the head should have been obvious to anyone. The hotel manager conceded that his wife occasionally caught her toe in the lion's head but was adamant that she had never fallen over it. The lion skin rug was in court, offering mute testimony from a table in front of the judge and jury. Mrs Neff claimed that it had constituted a concealed danger. The hotel's lawyers asked how she could have failed to notice the head. 'I never saw it until I was lying on the floor beside it,' Mrs Neff insisted.

• • •

IN June 1950, a farmer from Kirkcaldy mistakenly took medicine intended for one of his cows and gave the animal medicine he should have taken. The farmer recovered, but he had to call a vet to treat the cow.

• • •

OBAN sailor Ian McIntyre was tossing old newspapers, magazines and letters overboard the lighthouse supply ship in June 1971 when he realised (too late) that he had also just thrown his pay packet over the side of the ship. Inside the envelope was £19 in notes. He told his captain, Robert MacEachern, about his dreadful mistake. Captain MacEachern turned around the vessel at once and 'after a good mile and a half, one of the crew spotted the distinctive little green envelope bobbing on the waves'. A small boat was lowered and McIntyre's pay packet was successfully retrieved, to his relief and to the crew's amusement.

• • •

DUNDEE man Michael Chapman put his hand up a chimney in his house in November 1954 to try and find a loose draught plate and promptly got his arm stuck. No matter how hard Chapman tried, he was unable to free himself; neither could his wife, who called the fire brigade. Three firemen lifted Chapman upside down by his legs, but he still remained firmly stuck. They finally managed to free him after knocking bricks out of the wall, ending Chapman's ordeal after being trapped for over an hour.

• • •

IN June 1996, a couple ended up handcuffed together after a prank went wrong. Paul Murphy and Jennifer Sipple were colleagues behind the bar of an Edinburgh nightclub.

'Paul decided to have a joke and put one of the handcuffs on my wrist,' Jennifer explained. 'He was laughing and daring me to put one of the cuffs on him, so I did. Then we realised there weren't any keys.' They walked to a nearby fire station and begged the amused firemen to cut them free. Cutting equipment had to be brought to the station and the pair were released after the fireman had checked with the police to make sure the couple were not on the run. They had been handcuffed together for six hours.

• • •

DURING the Napoleonic Wars, there was a threat that France might invade Britain and Ireland, so a system of early warning lookouts was established along the coastlines of both islands. On the night of 31 January 1804, a sergeant on duty at Hume Castle in Berwickshire mistook the flickering fires of charcoal burners at work on the Cheviot Hills for an invasion beacon and ordered the castle's own beacon to be lit to raise the alarm. As a result, other beacons in the chain were lit across southern Scotland and 3,000 volunteers raised arms and prepared to fight a French invasion force. The force never arrived. The incident became known as 'The Great Alarm'. To save face, authorities declared that the false alarm was a demonstration of Scottish loyalty and an indication of their readiness to do battle with the enemy.

• • •

THE bizarre tale of twenty-three-year-old Alistair Nicholson from Glasgow became public knowledge in January 1948. Nicholson's saga began June 1947 when he ordered coffee instead of tea in a Southampton cafe, arousing the curiosity of an American army officer who was dining nearby. He accused the Scotsman of being an American seaman who had jumped ship. Nicholson protested, but was arrested by American military police who decided that he was a deserter from the American army. They would not believe that he was British, pointing out that he had no British accent.

After persistent questioning, Nicholson gave up in despair and told his interrogators that he indeed was an American army deserter, giving them a fictitious name and serial number. He fed them an outlandish account of his military career in the hope they would see through his lies and realise their mistake. Instead, the military accepted Nicholson's story at face value. A court-martial followed in Paris and Nicholson was jailed for three months and fined $99.

On his release, the Scotsman was deported 'home' to the United States in September 1946. Two months later the 'accidental soldier' was discharged from the army and paid off. Nicholson received $1,257.31 in back pay, $300 in mustering-out pay, $14.50 in travel pay and $920 in servicemen's readjustment allowance, all of which totalled just under $2,500. Nicholson told reporters that he thought the lies he had spun were so outrageous, the army would finally believe that he was telling the truth. He used the money to tour America, before heading home to Scotland.

•   •   •

FROGMEN from the frigate *Verulan* successfully retrieved Charles Tait's false teeth when they dived off the Shetland

Islands searching for them in May 1966. Tait, a fisherman, had lost his false teeth when he sneezed and they shot overboard.

• • •

EDINBURGH firemen were hugely embarrassed in August 1969 when they were called out after a man reported smoke pouring from a building. Wearing masks and prepared for the hazardous task ahead, the firefighters broke into the warehouse and discovered that it was empty. It was being fumigated for moths.

• • •

PRINCE Charles blushed but said nothing when a top Scottish businessman blundered and made a toast to the 'Prince Charles and Lady Jane', while wishing Charles and Lady Diana Spencer well on their engagement at a Glasgow business lunch on 26 February 1981. Afterwards, Peter Balfour, chairman of the Scottish Council for Development and Industry and chairman of Scottish and Newcastle Breweries said, 'I feel bloody awful, a perfect fool!' The Lady Jane in Charles's life was ex-girlfriend Lady Jane Wellesley, rumoured in 1974 to be his intended bride.

• • •

IN January 2003, crossing patrol staff at a Glasgow primary school were told by the city council that their pay slips could be provided in Braille if they were visually impaired.

• • •

SIR Arthur Conan Doyle, the Edinburgh-born writer most famous for his creation Sherlock Holmes, often played cricket for the MCC. In *Memories and Adventures*, he describes one unusual incident. Batting for the MCC against Kent, Conan Doyle was facing Kent's Walter Bradley, reputedly one of the fastest bowlers of the day.

'His first delivery I hardly saw, and it landed with a terrific thud upon my thigh,' Doyle wrote. 'A little occasional pain is one of the chances of cricket, and one takes it as cheerfully as one can, but on this occasion it suddenly became sharp to an unbearable degree. I clapped my hand to the spot, and found to my amazement that I was on fire. The ball had landed straight on a small tin vesta box in my trousers pocket, had splintered the box, and set the matches ablaze.' Conan Doyle quickly pulled out the burning matchbox and threw it onto the grass. Amongst the amused onlookers was Doyle's team mate, famous cricketer W.G. Grace, who quipped, 'Couldn't get you out – had to set you on fire.'

• • •

IN 1966, Pipe Major Iain McLeod of the Edinburgh City Police Band recorded four bagpipe tunes on tape. The tape was sent to a London record company, which produced and distributed 1,000 long-playing records. When a copy was sent to the Pipe Major, an incredible blunder was discovered. The bagpipe music on the record was playing backwards. The mistake had occurred after the master tape had been made from a tape that had accidentally been played in reverse. Over 400 copies had been sold before McLeod spotted the mistake. Worse still, not a single buyer complained.

• • •

AN accident left Glasgow man Gordon McLeod 'flush'. In July 1960, a court awarded him £472 damages when a public toilet he had sat on collapsed.